"Thanks, I Needed That"

THE BEGINNER'S NATURAL FOOD COOKBOOK

Thanks, I Needed That

The Beginner's Natural Food Cookbook

Judith Goeltz
and
Patricia Lazenby

Published by

Hawkes Publishing, Inc.

3775 South 500 West
Salt Lake City, Utah 84115
Phone: (801)-262-5555

Copyright© 1975
by Hawkes Publishing Inc.

ISBN 0-89036-048-0

First Printing, May, 1975

Typesetting
by
HAWKES PUBLISHING INC.

Foreword

At last, a book has been published for which my patients and many others have been waiting! It comes to us like a breath of pure, fresh, high-mountain air to help remove a lot of the cobwebs from an area of nutritional therapy which is often fraught with misconceptions and seeming contradictions. Judy Goeltz and Pat Lazenby, two of the most vibrant, healthy, and energetic young women anyone would ever hope to meet, have compiled a delightful and highly useful volume which will be an answer to many an anguished cry of frustration and bewilderment from individuals who have been diagnosed as being subject to the ravages of the hypoglycemic syndrome. When the diagnoses is first confirmed, all too often is heard such negative, though sincere, expressions as: "I'm certainly relieved to know what the cause of my symptoms is, but now what do I do? The doctor has taken me off of everything I eat! What am I going to do? What can I eat? What can I feed my family? It's all so confusing!" Fortunately, a carefully formulated and well planned book has now been written which will give hypoglycemics and others some really choice insights into the basic rules for good nutrition, as well as some sound advice on the selection, preparation, and storage of various kinds of food.

Judy and Pat, I thank you; my wife, Marian, thanks you; and thousands of others will also thank you for your efforts in making our daily task of eating not only one that will promote buoyant, abundant health, but one that will also make eating a fun and highly-pleasurable *nutritional* experience.

Robert Bliss Vance, D.O.

Contents

Section I
Introduction

Thanks, I Needed That! 17
The Philosophy of Balance 21

Section II
"No-No" Foods

Sugar, the Unfood 29
But We Eat Very Little Sugar 37
White flour and White Bread 38
Oils 41
Salt 42
Preservatives and
    Other Additives 45

Section III
Getting Down to the Basics

Protein 51
Preparation Time and
    Natural Food Cooking 54
Health Food Costs So Much 55
Weight Control 56
Proper Cooking Methods 57
Health Food Stores 59
Basics 60
Seeds 65
Wheat Germ 65
Nutritional Yeast 66

Bone Meal 67
Lecithin 68
Cheese 68
Yogurt 70
Honey 71

Section IV
Helps & Hints

What to Throw Out 79
Message to Hypoglycemics 80
Suggested Reading 83
Ecology Now 84
Steaming Vegetables 86
Sprouts 87
Beverages 89
Preserves 93

Section V
Recipes and Planned Meals

Breakfasts (day 1 - day 16) 99
Lunches 110
Breads 124
Dinners (day 1 - day 30) 131
Extra Main Dishes 178

Section I
Introduction

INTRODUCTION

THANKS, I NEEDED THAT!

People want to eat better, but they don't know where to start. Full-fledged "health food" has a slightly mysterious and dubious aura about it, while health food stores are interesting, but somewhat strange with their shelves of groats, brewers yeast, cayenne, bone meal, lentils and kelp. What does it all mean? What are they for? How do you eat them? What's good and what's bad and what's a fad of the day?

Your authors spent years and many dollars in doctors' offices trying to find a solution to our numerous and nearly continuous ailments, with little success and plenty of misery. Finally we found a doctor who understood the importance of nutrition for a healthy body, and who believed in preventive medicine rather than in simply treating symptoms with medication. He looked for the cause, and found that we had low blood sugar, hypoglycemia, or if you want to be more medical about it, hypoadrenocorticism. We left the doctor's office relieved to have at last found the source of our problems, but dismayed by the restrictive diet given us. We looked ahead grimly at the limited diet we would be consuming for the rest of our lives.

Then we began reading, studying and looking for new ways to eat what we enjoyed—foods that would build us up rather than destroy our bodies. We discovered that we could eat nearly all the foods denied us, if they were prepared carefully and properly, (and, since we had low blood sugar, eaten only in small amounts at first until a tolerance was built up for these foods as our bodies became more healthy). The only restrictions we followed adamantly were the use of processed foods, nutrient-poor and full of chemicals to preserve and color, the use of white sugar and white flour, and the "no-no" foods improperly prepared.

We do not believe in negative dietetics. Negative dietetics tells you what not to eat, and is almost routinely productive of poor nutrition because it is unbalanced. We don't believe that a body can grow healthy and function properly by restricting natural foods which contain vitamins and minerals, enzymes and protein, fats and carbohydrates—all needed in complementary amounts by the body to work and grow. We believe that the key to good eating is BALANCE, which we get with natural, living foods, properly prepared.

There are extremes (extreme need not connote negativism) among health food fans. We would like to be an introdution to natural eating without throwing you into a totally strange world of funny tastes and textures. We are not vegetarians, though some prefer not to eat meat because it is mucous-forming, not easily digested, and apparently tastes good to cancerous cells. We have recipes for pork, which many consider a wormy, fatty, hard-to-digest protein. We include salt (sea salt), and natural sweeteners such as honey and sorghum, though many oppose any form of sweetener or salt, preferring the pure taste of the food. We don't recommend that all food be eaten raw, though there are those who feel that any cooking whatever "kills" the food—that cooked food is no longer living food for a living body. This is not to say that all these people don't have good reasons for their preferences. There are a great many controversies and contradictions in the area of health foods. We will let you know what they are whenever possible, and you can make up your mind for yourself.

Meanwhile, we help to be a stepping stone for you. We want to introduce you to natural-food cooking with dishes that taste pretty much like the ones you and your family (the really hard ones to convince) are used to, though the flavors won't be so bland. Many full-fledged natural food recipes can taste pretty strange before a taste for them has been developed. We hope to bridge that gap for you. If you follow our thoughts and recipes, and go no further, we believe you will be more healthy, and if you decide to investigate further you will do it with some basic knowledge and developed taste for natural foods.

To help you we've included some basics for the kitchen, and explanations of why refined foods, especially sugar and flour, are so bad for the body. You will become a discerning reader of labels. And there are menus with recipes to get you started. By the time you finish trying our menus, you should be ready to branch out on your own, to adapt your recipes into healthier food, and to create your own dishes.

There is also an important section on cooking preparation. To our knowledge this has not been discussed in other cookbooks, and we consider it essential to maintaining a balance of the nutrients in the food. We have found that many foods we prepare at home we are able to eat with no ill effects, but the same foods are intolerable to our bodies when eaten in restaurants or in other homes where these cooking techniques are not followed. Of course, we have an immediate gauge telling us how the food is affecting our bodies. Since we are hypoglycemic, our bodies react almost immediately with stuffy noses and headaches or stomach aches to unbalanced, high-carbohydrate foods.

In fact we have become adamant followers of proper eating habits. We spent so many years dragging our tired, totally fatigued bodies around, catching every virus and every cold that came our way, and some that didn't come our way. We remember, too, panting to climb a small hill. Hiking or skiing at high altitudes caused nausea and headaches, and even the slightest noise would be like a sharp knife scratching slowly across a slate board, because our nerves weren't being fed. Our B-vitamins were used up in sugar digestion, and we were deficient in nearly every mineral as well as vitamin.[1]

We don't claim that food alone changed all this. We were too far gone. We had to take mega-supplements of vitamins and minerals (without minerals the vitamins won't be assimilated), and even had some vitamin injections. That was

---

1. With poor nutrition, a vicious cycle is set up. Dr. Carlton Fredericks explains this cycle in *Food Facts and Fallacies* (New York: Julian Press, Inc.) Individual nutritional needs vary enormously from one person to the next, and in one person from time to time. Poor nutrition is part of an inevitable cycle. At the outset it debilitates the pituitary gland, which influences the enzyme systems through which nutrients are utilized. Thus, as deficiency lowers the efficiency of the gland, digestion, absorption, utilization and formation of enzyme systems will, in comparable

for the "healing" process. Once the body is fairly healthy, a good, nutrient-balanced, natural diet should maintain good health.

Many people claim that they are never sick. Somehow they don't count the colds and sore throats we see them suffering from. I see young children with serious problems like asthma being put on restrictive diets, which to our way of thinking can only increase the problem through a resulting deficiency, since much evidence points to deficiency as the possible cause of the illness to begin with. We see people suffer from respiratory infection for weeks and sometimes months, but not be concerned enough to stop eating the junk clogging up their systems and depleting its reserves, thus producing a delightful home for those viruses.

It is bad enough seeing women and men our age panting after us as we climb a hill, but sadder yet is the child deprived of good health because the parents are either unknowledgeable, and/or unwilling to spend the little extra time to learn to feed that child properly. The fat, soft youngsters we see around us are increasing in number. We are looking at carbohydrate fat— the result of highly processed foods where all the life-building nutrients have been destroyed in favor of appearance, convenience, longer shelf life and marketability of the food. With only dead carbohydrates entering a body, the child is left starving. He seems to eat enough quantity of food, but it only satisfies the hunger temporarily while the carbohydrates rapidly drive his blood sugar up.

These children have colds, flu and sore throats all winter. Many of them become either apathetic or hyperactive or both in school, which parents and authorities treat, if they treat at all, with counseling and/or drugs. Unexplainable fits of crying or outbursts of rage are considered emotional problems. These children are nutritionally deprived and need to have their diets checked. More concern is taken in "feeding" the family car the proper fuels and lubricants than is used in fueling the human

_____

degree, suffer impairment. The very nutrients needed to stimulate the pituitary are utilized with steadily-decreasing effectiveness, and the gland continues to go downhill. An individual suffering from this condition frequently refuses to respond to therapeutic dosages of the nutrients he apparently needs.

child for optimum body efficiency. Such children should be taken to qualified doctors who will check specifically for vitamin, mineral and protein deficiencies. These children should stop eating white sugar, white flour and sandwich meats loaded with indigestible chemicals, and let's face it, poisons.

We suppose people just aren't convinced of the seriousness of diet, and that is easy to understand. Heaven knows our culture and food processors and drug firms daily proclaim that we are all healthy and our average diet is healthy and could not produce deficiencies.[2] We believe that a proper diet is integral to a healthy body. Food and supplements made such a difference in our lives that it hurts to see others suffer through ignorance, laziness, or misguidance. But, we allow each his free agency and his choice of diet. After all, a person has a right to be sick.) If we can help a few of our readers take the first step towards healthier eating and better nutrition, we will consider our efforts in producing this book rewarded.

THE PHILOSOPHY OF BALANCE

Our philosophy of eating is expressed in one word: BALANCE. It makes sense that a part missing from the whole will be missed by the whole resulting in disharmony at best, and in failure to perform at worst. When that missing part is restored we again see the harmony of the whole.

We have been criticized for attributing the cause of most problems, physical and mental, to deficiencies. We may be wrong and too enthusiastic, but we may be right. Here's what Gena Larson, cafeteria manager of the Helix High School of San Diego County, California managed to accomplish with nutrition.[3] The school lunch program was changed to include liberal supplements added to the food, such as wheat germ, bone meal, soy flour and rice polish. Dessert was a choice of

---

2. "But in fact we are getting shorter and there is a greater problem of overweight and underweight." Mark Bricklin, *Prevention*, Sept., 1973, pp. 134, 135.

3. Gena Larson is a monthly contributor to the health magazine *Let's Live*.

frozen orange juice bar, gelatin or fresh fruit. Other regulars contained good food values, including raw carrots, celery, apples, boysenberry and orange juices. Their snacks were raisins, sunflower seeds, pumpkin seeds and wheat germ flakes. The results were applauded by the California Youth Authority. They claimed improved dental health (fewer cavities), better emotional health, better citizenship and better grades, including an answer to the drop-out problem. And all this was accomplished while the students still ate their regular diets while away from school.

There is a lot more testing and research to be done in this field and at present there are contradictions and disagreements in many areas of natural health among the natural health specialists themselves. But it would be absurd to wait until all the facts are in. Eating better cannot hurt us, even if it is someday proven (which we doubt) that good eating has no relationship to good health. We are guided by our own experiences. Our multiple aches and pains and complaints and depressions and illnesses, unexplainable by many doctors in many parts of the country, disappeared, some suddenly, some gradually, when we began to avoid processed, refined, chemically-laden foods and began to eat whole, living foods, combined with supplements to build up very damaged bodies. Apparently deficiency was the key to our problems. We were raised on typical American food and came from middle class families not considered "deprived" in any way. If this could happen to us, why not to others? We believe it has happened and is happening to others, if even to a slight degree.

Dr. Fredericks points out that the general medical concept of deficiency is all or nothing. If you don't have scurvy, then you are getting enough vitamin C.[4] They fail to take into account the twilight zone of deficiency where the person has enough of a mineral or vitamin to prevent clinical signs of the extreme deficiency of the substance, but not enough to enable the

---

4. The recommended daily allowance as determined by the Food and Drug Administration (FDA) is based on the amount of a particular vitamin, e. g. vitamin B, necessary to prevent the "average" person from getting pellagra. It is not based on optimum health, nor could it be since individual needs vary so much. Needs vary from time to time within the same person. Stress can greatly heighten the need for vitamins.

person to live to his optimum health. The person is neither sick nor well, and the vague complaints and illnesses are credited to psychosomatic origins, or are simply considered unimportant. This is like saying that a fire must burst through the roof before we grant that a disaster is in progress (Dr. Fredericks' comparison). This is saying that a person who has purple tongue, cracks at the corners of the mouth, diarrhea, skin distrubances and delirium has pellegra and is therefore deficient, but that during the years preceding the emergence of this disease there were no deviations from the norm of physical and mental health, that there was no deficiency, and that therefore all can be ignored.

A doctor who is truly concerned about nutrition can make the proper tests. (More than a blood test is needed. Often there are sufficient nutrients in the blood stream which are not absorbed by the body for one reason or another, and they never reach the cells. The tests should involve activity at the cellular level. One such test is made on a large hunk of hair.) Then the doctor can prescribe just what the individual needs, and he will make sure that the supplements are properly balanced. Some vitamins cannot work without others present (this goes for minerals, too), and he is qualified to make sure all the complements are there.[5]

And then eat a truly balanced diet. We don't recommend restriction of any foods except the refined, processed non-foods. We eat saturated fats. It has never been proven that cholesterol causes arterial problems, nor that a diet that includes saturated fats causes these problems. What has happened it seems, is that someone noticed that cholesterol was present in arterial and heart problems. They reasoned that

---

5. When we say "qualified doctor" we mean just that. Not all medical doctors are qualified in the realm of nutrition. They have had very little training in it, and are oriented toward treating symptons rather than toward preventive medicine. Check your doctor out carefully. If he is honest, an untrained doctor will admit that he has had very little training in nutrition. The doctor who knows little about nutrition but won't admit it often covers his ignorance by making fun of the importance of nutrition, and/or claims one's problems are "all in the head."

if one avoided eating cholesterol, then the problems would cease. They didn't prove a causal relationship. They didn't take into account that cholesterol is a vitally needed substance and if the body doesn't get enough of it, it will manufacture its own, that it is impossible to eliminate cholesterol from the diet, since the body converts vegetable fat into the animal type and can make cholesterol from starch, sugar and any kind of fat.

They accused eggs and warned us not to eat them, failing to acknowledge that eggs contain unsaturated as well as saturated fats, and that they are rich in lecithin, the cholesterol emulsifier and the antagonistic-yet-synergistic phospholipid partner of cholesterol. They didn't mention that eggs are also rich in choline, inositol, pyridoxine, all of which are used, along with lecithin, in medical treatment of hardening of the arteries.[6] In fact, it has been found that if the body has enough of the substances called phospholipids, they act in dynamic equilibrium with the cholesterol to maintain the integrity of each cell. (Eggs are probably also the most nutritious staple food available, milk being second. And in terms of net protein usability, eggs rank the highest.) We cannot live without a supply of cholesterol, and to exclude it is running the risk of malnutrition so bad that life can no longer be supported and the person dies before there is time for hardening of any arteries to occur. Elimination of cholesterol from the diet does not seem to have affected the number of people who still die from heart disease, and is a very simplistic approach at best, based on no hard evidence and ignoring the resulting effects on nutrition.[7]

In fact, recent tests have pointed the finger to sugar and other over-processed carbohydrates as the real villains. The electron microscope has taught that the initial invader of the artery wall may not be cholesterol at all, but an abnormal sugar-protein molecule. It is on a plaque of these abnormal

---

6. While eggs are rich in fat and cholesterol, they are also high in antidotes which are prescribed for prevention and treatment of hardening of the arteries. The egg is a well-balanced food in this respect.

7. Cholesterol is necessary as a raw material in the production of female sex hormones.

molecules that cholesterol begins to deposit. There are several papers indicating that the kind and amounts of starch and sugar in the diet may be more relevant to the problem than the quantity or the chemistry of the fats.[8]

Another vitamin that is important in controlling cholesterol levels is vitamin C. Tests in guinea pigs, one of the few animals that, like humans, do not produce their own vitamin C, showed that a relative deficiency in vitamin C produced an increase in cholesterol. Further investigation showed the increase to be due to the inability of the liver in the absence of vitamin C, to oxidize excess cholesterol into bile acids. which are then eliminated from the body, causing an accumulation of cholesterol and triglycerides in the liver and the blood. A correlation analysis study on human beings in which vitamin C intake and ischemic heart disease and cerebrovascular disease were linked, showed a lower rate of death from both diseases where vitamin C intake was high.[9]

We also need to consider that the thyroid gland has a lot to do with controlling blood cholesterol and influencing tissue cholesterol. Dr. Fredricks points out that a chronic mild deficiency of vitamin B, so easily possible in a sugar-saturated public, can cause thyroid underactivity and a consequent elevation of blood cholesterol.

Since vitamin B is used up by the body during assimilation of sugar and processed carbohydrates, since vitamin B is needed to maintain a healthy thyroid which in turn regulates cholesterol, and since vitamin B-6 is removed from white

---

8. Dr. John Yudkin, professor of Nutrition at Queen Elizabeth College, cites the triglyceride levels in the blood, which sugar tends to raise, as more critical indices of susceptibility to cardiac disease than cholesterol levels are. He says that low triglyceride and high cholesterol levels do NOT increase risk of heart disease; that high triglyceride levels and low cholesterol levels DO increase that rate, while high levels of both are a strong invitation to heart attack. *Prevention* (February, 1974), pp. 69, 70.

9. Dr. Emil Ginter, "Vitamin C Protects Against High Blood Cholesterol," *Prevention* (February, 1974), pp. 74-80.

bread[10] and not restored, we might do well to eliminate white flour products as well as sugar from our diets. It was found that cholesterol intake had little effect on the arteries of monkeys, unless they were deprived of vitamin B-6.

Dr. Roger J. Williams (Ph. D) recommends that since lecithin emulsifies or homogenizes the cholesterol in the blood, we shouldn't shun cholesterol but "consume more lecithin." Dr. Fredricks indicates that the problem may be due to a B-vitamin deficiency brought on by over-consumption of sugar and over-processed, depleted carbohydrates, which in turn affects the thyroid gland. This means that we must maintain an adequate supply of the B-vitamin complex. One further note is that the lower incidence of heart and arterial problems in women has been attributed to the estrogenic hormone. Vitamin E has certain effects resembling those of the estrogenic hormone. It is not uncommon to have vitamin E recommended to men as a heart problem preventative.

What this all adds up to is balance. Don't worry about the consumption of cholesterol-producing foods, but be sure to maintain a balance. Include sufficient vitamin B, vitamin C, and vitamin E, as well as lecithin in the diet, while avoiding white sugar and the processed carbohydrates that have been depleted of these nutrients.[11] Make sure that there is balance in your diet.

Since our concept of diet is based upon balance, we feel that *Thanks, I Needed That* can be a very satisfactory book for hypoglycemics. Most such cookbooks would exclude all carbohydrates, or include only some natural ones. We fear elimination could cause (or continue) deficiency, so we include carbohydrates in the form of fresh fruits and vegetables, in whole grains and cereals, in honey and molasses. *If they are "whole" and properly cooked* (this cannot be emphasized enough), a hypoglycemic, except in the very beginning recuperative stages or one with extremely low blood sugar, should be able to tolerate the foods we include.

---

10. Lecithin and other lipotropic factors which help us to utilize fats are also removed.

11. Pasteurizing milk destroys the lecithin, so we recommend raw milk. And we far prefer the natural animal fat, butter, to its cheaper, petroleum-based counterpart.

Section II
"No-No" Foods

Section II

"NO-NO" FOODS
SUGAR, THE UNFOOD

"Sugar is a starvation food," says Dr. Phillip M. Lovell in his column in the *Los Angeles Times*. "It's physiological effect on the body has been demonstrated again and again . . . . in the technical manufacture of sugar, it becomes devitalized, demineralized, and robbed of any life-giving qualities it once possessed."

Sugar is one thing: it is pure. And the purity of sugar is its danger. Nature doesn't want fragmentation, or a single compound by itself. It wants wholeness, a package deal, a compound surrounded by vitamins and minerals. The sugar molecule is always something like Cn-$H2n$-On (carbon, hydrogen and oxygen). It isn't a food, but rather a chemical compound. And when injested, because it is water soluble, it rushes rampaging into the bloodstream without spending much time in the digestive tract. Dr. Victor Lorenc says, "This sugar is a soluble food of which nothing slows down the delivery. It falls into the intestine as though from a waterspout, transforms itself in a twinkling of an eye into glucose, and overexcites the intestinal villi, which send it *en masse* to the liver. Now the liver has been conditioned by a thousand years in the past which knew nothing at all of the avalanches of glucose let loose by today's industrial sugar. Thus the liver cannot prevent a temporary excess of sugar in the blood. Each cell of the body will have to suffer for this defeat, including those of the liver itself."[1]

---

1. "White Sugar and Its Effects on the Body," *La Vie Claire*.

Sugar, 99 per cent sucrose, is a foodless food, and potentially dangerous when eaten. It is empty calories, not an energy food. In fact, it robs the body of the B vitamins,[2] disrupts calcium and protein metabolism, and is harmful to the nervous system.

The nerves need vitamin B to remain healthy. Think of the B vitamins as food for the nerves. These vitamins are also required by the body for digestion of sugar. Natural sugars like raw honey, molasses or date sugar contain their own B vitamins as well as other natural minerals and enzymes needed for their digestion, so their assimilation is not a strain on the body. But white, refined sugar is nearly pure carbon, with all original enzymes and minerals and vitamins removed. When it enters the body, it must steal the necessary B vitamins that the body is storing for other uses. It is, in effect, stealing food from the nerves.

Even then the sugar is often not properly metabolized. The removal during refinement of the required vitamin and mineral catalysts interferes with the metabolism, resulting in the production of toxic metabolites. Tests show that these metabolites from the incomplete carbohydrate metabolism interfere with cellular oxidation, which results in the formation of abnormal cells. This is the beginning of tissue pathology.[3]

"Granulated or white sugar is deficient in organic salts because of the process of refining, and when taken into the body breaks down the cells in order to furnish the blood with the necessary alkaline elements to neutralize the carbonic acid which is formed by the oxidation of the carbon, of which sugar is composed. Sugar is almost pure carbon."[4]

According to E. G. White, sugar ". . . clog[s] the system, irritate[s] the digestive organs, and affect[s] the brain. Anything that hinders the active motion of the living machinery affects the brain very directly."

---

2. J. I. Rodale, *Natural Health, Sugar and the Criminal Mind* (New York: Pyramid Books) p. 25.

3. Dr. W. Coda Martin, address to Friends of the Land (Chicago, June 26, 1956.)

4. Remsburg, *Pan American Diet Book*.

When people ask Linda Clarke, noted nutritionist, what's wrong with sugar she answers, "Everything is wrong with sugar, particularly refined white sugar. Just to name a few things, it steals B vitamins from the body, causes dental decay, is incriminated in heart disease, is a major factor in hypoglycemia. Yes, it provides energy because it raises the blood sugar, but immediately afterward the rise is followed by a nose dive of the blood sugar, which gets you permanently hooked on sugar.[5] It is also considered by many to be a major cause of diabetes."She then points out that Dr. Jin Otsuka, Professor of Opthamalogy, Tokyo Medical and Dental University, has produced myopia, or near-sightedness in rabbits by feeding them sugar.[6]

She might have added these other health problems to her list: multiple sclerosis, tongue ulcers, periodontitis, headaches, sinusitis, dandruff, constipation, high blood pressure, polio, exhaustion, boils, ulcers, tonsilitis, cancer, cholesterol, heart disease and menstrual pain. Sugar is implicated in all of them. Let's look into some of the studies done regarding these problems and their relation to sugar.

Dandruff has been cured by a no-sugar diet and B-vitamin therapy. Besides evidence that excessive sucrose intake causes seborrheic dermatitis, Dr. Yudkin points out that eaten on an empty stomach it can seriously disrupt hormone levels, which could be one explanation why elimination of sugar from the diet has been known to "cure" menstrual cramps.

People who eat cane sugar or sweetmeats to excess often complain of sour stomach or acidity. These acids are formed from the decomposition of the sugar with meats or other proteins. The chief acid formed is oxalic acid. Sugar added to a low carbohydrate diet triples production of stomach acid and the enzyme pepsin, resulting in levels that make for stomach

---

5. It is a vicious circle. The yen for sweets is, in fact, not the sign of insufficient intake of sweets, but, on the contrary, is already the result of too much sugar consumption. The system inaugurates an abnormal drop of the blood sugar which, in turn, causes an unnatural craving for something sweet.

6. *Let's Live* (September, 1972), p. 123.

ulcers. When it reaches the blood it converts the soluble lime salts into insoluble oxalate of lime, inducing the condition known as decalcification or lime starvation, which can lead to catarrh or rheumatism, dilated or catarrhal stomachs, rickets, decay of teeth, adenoid nasal growth and inflamed tonsils.

As for polio, Dr. Benjamin P. Sandler was quite successful in greatly diminishing the number of cases of polio in the summer of 1946 with specific dietary recommendations eliminating all sugar and cutting down on starchy foods like white flour, while he urged consumption of green vegetables and lots of protein. He explains that the infection with the poliomyelitis virus is only possible if the blood sugar level goes below 80 mg per cent temporarily.[7]

Sugar has been indicated as a possible indirect factor in cancer. It is known that cancer sufferers in the final stages and right up to the point of death can be free of pain if they eat only natural foods and eliminate all artificial sugar and products containing this sugar. Excessive use of sugar causes a complete imbalance in the tissue cells, and in strong solution is an irritant to the tissues. This stress, plus the stress of malnourishment due to the nature of sugar certainly couldn't help any illness, and could logically, it seems, promote or enhance an illness already in the body.

Repeatedly sugar is implicated in heart and cholesterol problems. In a study done on the average American diet over the past seventy years, it was discovered that the fat consumption had increased by only 12 per cent, most of the increase being of polyunsaturated fats. Since it is widely believed that ischaemic heart disease is caused by a low ratio of polyunsaturated fat to saturated fat, we could expect to see a fall in the prevalence of ischaemic heart disease, but in fact, there has been a considerable rise; and the major dietary changes during the same period were a decrease in the consumption of starchy foods, and an increase of as much as 120 per cent in the consumption of sugar.[8]

----

7. Dr. Benjamin P. Sandler, *Diet Prevents Polio* (Milwaukee: Lee Foundation for Nutritional Research.)

8. Dr. Yudkin, *Natural Health, Sugar and the Criminal Mind* (New York: Pyramid Books), p. 159.

According to the prominent nutritionists Walter H. Eddy, PhD, and Gilbert Dalldorf, MD, "Thiamin deficiency impairs the function of the heart, increases the tendency to extravascular fluid collections and results in terminal cardiac standstill."[9] We know that consumption of table sugar uses thiamin from the body and does not replace it, which can easily lead to a thiamin deficiency. Dr. Yudkin found that "patients who had recently had an infarct (heart attack) had been consuming twice as much sugar as the control subjects."[10] He feels that this is strong evidence that sugar is a cause of myocardial infarction, and he is backed up by three doctors from Czechoslovakia who believe that excess consumption of sugar, not fat, is associated with increasing heart disease.[11]

Finally, let's look at this possible source of cholesterol. An article entitled "White Sugar and Its Effects on the Body" by Dr. Victor Lorenc, published in a French health magazine called *La Vie Claire* discusses fat globules caused by sugar. It explains that sugar brings a brutally copious afflux of glucose to the liver, which stores as much of it as it can. Nevertheless, it cannot hold more than 150 grams of glycogen, so it transforms the excessive glycogen into fat globules, which are distributed a bit here and there throughout the body, especially in regions where the muscles do little work.

In test animals, dietary sucrose produced an accumulation of fats in the aorta, and in human testing, men showed an increase in cholesterol levels, as well as levels of blood fats and platelet stickiness.

It isn't only that sugar increases vitamin needs or lowers the supply; it actually causes changes in the blood chemistry of the type physicians consider to increase the rate of heart disease. In a paper presented to the International Academy of Preventive Medicine, Dr. John Yudkin made these points in relation to sugar consumption: adhesion of blood platelets increases; liver cells increase indefinitely; adrenal cells increase, but not indefinitely; in test animals sugar directly causes atheromatous lesions in the aorta; aortal level of fatty

---

9. Ibid., p. 160.

10. Ibid., p. 160.

11. Ibid., p. 160.

acids and cholesterol rise; the body goes into a negative nitrogen balance, indicating tissue breakdown; glucose tolerance becomes abnormal; cortisol levels rise, indicating a stress reaction conducive to decalcification.[12]

Throughout this chapter we have been talking about processed or refined sugar. Here's what is involved in the process.

In the case of sugar cane, the agricultural processes are destructive from the outset. The cane is grown with the use of synthetic fertilizers and weed sprays. Then the fields are burned right before harvest. With soil so mistreated it would be difficult for it to nourish the living cane.

The refining of cane sugar includes boiling, spinning, filtering, and separating the sugar in huge machines at high heat. In the process, water, lime, phosphoric acid and diatamaceous earth are added to the sugar. We needn't really worry about these additives, though, because nothing is left of them at the end of the process. As we have said before, sugar is pure.

In processing sugar beets, the important salts are removed when the tops and small part of the neck are removed. Then lime or carbon dioxide is added to precipitate some impurities before it is centrifuged, separating the clear juice into molasses and raw beet sugar.

The raw beet sugar is heated thoroughly, destroying every particle of organized cell life in it. Next are added acid calcium phosphate, phosphoric acid, and milk of lime, and to carry away any suspended protein matter the manufacturer uses blood albumin from slaughter houses.

Animal charcoal, also from the slaughter houses, is used as a filter to help purify it, and the twice-heated sugar must be thoroughly boiled to separate it from the syrup. Finally, to make the sugar as white as possible, it is bleached with a strong bleaching agent—blue water in the case of first-grade sugar, or calcium and barium hydroxide in inferior sugars.

What of brown sugar? We should forget that too. Brown, dark brown, and Kleenraw sugar are all made the same way, by

---

12. Could this be related to the widespread osteoporosis (weakening of the bones) and periodontal disease (decalcification of the jawbone leading to loosening of the teeth) so common in our country?

adding molasses to the refined white sugar. Fred Rohe writes in *The Sugar Story*, "The numbers go like this: Partially refined or 'raw' sugar is 97 per cent sucrose when it leaves Hawaii and goes through a gigantic California refinery to produce refined sugar, which is 99.96 per cent sucrose. For Kleenraw they add back 5 per cent molasses, for light brown they add back 12 per cent molasses, and for dark brown they add back thirteen per cent molasses. A special crystallization process is used for Kleenraw designed especially to create a raw-like illusion."[13]

Yellow-D sugar is often used by natural food people, since they consider it preferable to other sugars, but it is still processed to some degree. (The FDA sees to that. The consumer has no choice.)

Occasionally Turbinado or Demarara sugar is sold in health food stores. Their use is up to you, of course. We believe that since the government requires all sugar to be refined to some degree, then these, too, must refined. Mr. Rohe refuses to sell either of those. He says, "I have not seen Turbinado or Demarara sugar produced, but my understanding of sugar processing enables me to make the following wager with complete confidence: I'll bet Turbinado sugar is at least 95 per cent sucrose . . . . That wager makes no pretense of being founded on 'scientific' grounds, but on first-hand experience of what sugar looks like during the refining procedure."

Who needs sugar anyway? Artificial sweeteners taste fine and have fewer calories.

Watch out! Most artificial sweeteners are made from coal tar derivatives. The human body was not built to digest coal tar, so where should we suppose it goes once it enters the body?

Coal heated to the proper temperature becomes coke, and coal tar. By fractional distillation of the tar, some basic compounds, all deadly poisons, appear: benzene, toluene, xylene, phenol, creosote, naphtha and carbolic acid. These basic compounds are then used to manufacture food colorings, some medicinal drugs, perfumes, flavorings, disinfectants, preservatives, photographic chemicals, various barbituric acids for sleeping pills, and saccharin.

---

13. Erewhon, *The Sugar Story* (Culver City, California: Erewhon Trading Co.) pamph.

It is a well-recognized medical fact that prolonged use of saccharin can damage the liver,[14] and tests done on rabbits, motivated by a doctor who found that decreased intake of saccharin seemed to reduce goiters in his patients, showed that saccharin injections developed unhealthy, enlarged thyroid glands. The uninjected control group developed no thyroid problem.[15] Saccharin has been credited with being responsible for cases of dizziness, itching, unexplainable rashes, wooziness and ringing in the ears. Its laxative effect has been known for a long time. In a test in which dry peas were soaked in various solutions it was concluded that saccharin is a protoplasmic poison, and that regardless of how long the process may take, eventually saccharin poisons protoplasm, the very substance we are made of.[16]

Saccharin is also a powerful auxetic (which excites cell production), and there is strong evidence that it is these auxetics in tar and pitch that give rise to the predisposition to the cancer known as pitch and sweep's cancer.

Unlike many sugarless cooks, we do not recommend the use of artificial sweeteners. We use the natural, whole sweeteners like raw honey, unsulphured molasses, especially blackstrap (it has the highest mineral content), sorghum, maple syrup, date sugar, carob molasses and syrup, and real vanilla.

Ideally we should all cut down on the use of any added sweeteners to rid ourselves of the sweet-taste syndrome that we have developed since our first mouthful of baby food. As less sweetener is added to our food, we will desire it less and the fruits and vegetables and natural foods will taste sweet and satisfying to us.

---

14. Valentine and Weber, *Journal of Comparative Physiological Psychology*, pp. 443-446.

15. Imrich Molee, MD *Bratislovski Lekarske Listy* (Czechoslovakia:, May 1938.)

16. E. Verschaffelt, MD *Pharmaceutish Weekblad* (Dutch), LIX, 1915.

BUT WE EAT VERY LITTLE SUGAR

We hear this nearly every time we mention the apparent dangers of sugar consumption. In fact, we used to say it. But that was before we read labels on the foods we bought. Now that we do read labels, there is no way we could make such an absurd statement.

Try to find some foods in your supermarket that have neither a sugar nor a coal tar artificial sweetener added. Nearly all processed meats have sugar in them, crackers, mixed seasoning like seasoning salt, canned vegetables (and of course fruits), canned and dry soups, all have sugar in them. Even many frozen vegetables have sugar added. Foods that say "cured" are usually cured with sugar. Imitation dairy products for coffee, etc., have sugar in them. If the labels read caramel coloring, malt added, or corn syrup or dextrose, you have an item with sugar in it. Most leading brands of peanut butter have some form of sugar added, and so do most baby foods.

Margo Vlebin and Geri Ginder in the *Low Blood Sugar Cookbook* offer us a typical day's menu that the average housewife would feed her children:

For breakfast, she'd begin with an instant fruit drink (sugar), presweetened cereal (sugar, starch), with milk, toast (starch, sugar) and jam (sugar), and perhaps a cup of cocoa (sugar). Then on to lunch: a can of soup (sugar, starch), a sandwich of bologna (sugar, corn syrup solids, dextrose), two pieces of bread (starch, sugar) and mayonnaise (sugar). Milk or soda (sugar, possibly caffeine) just wouldn't taste right unless accompanied by cookies (starch, sugar), and possibly canned fruit (in thick sugar syrup). Dinner might consist of some frozen·fish cakes (starch, sugar), tartar sauce,(sugar), spaghetti (starch, sugar), sweet pickles (sugar), salad with bottled salad dressing (sugar), and canned peas. (sugar). Don't even mention dessert; it's about 90 per cent sugar, whatever it is. Later, there will be TV snacks of popcorn, (starch), pretzels (starch), and candy, for "energy" or reward.

In 1900, the average consumption of sugar in the United States per person per year was about nine pounds. Today it is over 150 pounds per person per year. Even families who never eat desserts consume large quantities of sugar, and will continue to do so until they become label readers, eliminating all processed foods containing sugar.

WHITE FLOUR AND WHITE BREAD

We should have become suspicious of white flour when we mixed it with water to make book paste and those relief maps in school. We never wondered how such glue could be absorbed by the body, or if it weren't absorbed, what happened to it.

How proud we would feel of the great American technology that so conscientiously removed the germs from our flour. That's what we thought "degerminated" meant.

Well, we've learned a lot. "Degerminated" means that the processors have removed the germ of the wheat kernel, or the wheat germ. It is the darkish speck about the size and shape of a pinhead found near the end of each kernel of wheat. Germ means heart, or essence of life, and the wheat germ is the heart of the seed of the wheat which, if planted, will send forth a sprout to grow into a new plant.

The germ is very important to health. Not only is it high in protein, but it contains many important enzymes, every known B vitamin, and practically all the required minerals. It appears to have a cholesterol-lowering effect, as well as an antibiotic and antihistamine effect for fighting allergies. It helps the body utilize fats and carbohydrates, and supports certain intestinal bacteria needed for B vitamin synthesis.

When wheat was stone-ground, the germ was pulverized, but since the introduction of the steel rollers around the turn of the century the germ goes through the rollers intact and is later sifted out of the flour. This was deemed beneficial by the food companies, since wheat germ, because it supports life, can spoil easily. With the germ removed, white flour and white flour products had a longer shelf life, spoilage decreased, it had longer staying qualities and could be shipped more readily around the world. It was commercially expedient to remove the germ.

What the processor gives back to us is "enriched" flour. This is funny, but sad. When they remove the germ and process the flour, 33 nutrients are removed, every one essential to maintaining a healthy system. Enrichment puts back 3 nutrients, in 1/3 the original amount, in synthetic form.[17]

Jane Kinderlehrer, in *Confessions of a Sneaky Organic Cook,* says it well:

> *"That word 'enriched' has been pulling the wool over our eyes and leading us down the path to deficiencies for too many years. Look at it this way. If someone stole your wallet with $200 in it, your favorite snapshots, credit cards, and drivers license, and returned your emptied wallet, license and 20 cents for car fare to you, would you consider yourself enriched?"*

The processing also removes the pantothenic acid. Symptoms of pantothenic acid deficiency are vague pains, neuritis, lack of energy, inability to think, lapses of memory, and in very serious deficiencies, apathy, depression, heart abnormalities, abdominal pain, susceptibility to infections, impairment of adrenal glands, and disorders of the nerves and muscles.

We've discussed what's been removed. Now let's look at what is added. Edward Marsh, in *How to Be Healthy With Natural Foods,* remarks that:

> *"The stomachs of many people are unable to handle [white] bread—starch—and no wonder when one realizes that our modern 'staff of life' contains sodium propionate to kill fungi, chlorine dioxide to bleach it, the jaw-breaking polhoxyethylene-monostearate to prevent staleness and keep it soft and fluffy, plus five or six other chemicals that are added to it at various points during its production."*

---

17. The controversy of natural versus artificial vitamins has not been settled. Dr. Carlton Fredericks in his book *Food Facts and Fallacies* claims that it has never been possible to demonstrate even an insignificant difference between their actions, so long as comparable products were being compared, though he does recommend a natural source of the B-vitamin complex, since we still don't know all the factors that make up the vitamin, and warns against using supplements in place of a good diet. Still, the controversy continues, and we leave it to the reader to decide for himself.

The description of additives to white bread is even more horrifying in the *Basic Book of Organically Grown Foods:*

Bread. This one is a chemist's dream. As a starter, the seed from which the wheat was grown was probably treated with bichloride of mercury—a dangerous poison with a rating of 5. As it grew, the grain was sprayed with a variety of pesticides with toxicity rating between 4 and 5. The flour was then bleached with agene, nitrogen trichloride, or chlorine dioxide. Agene was used for 25 years until the University of Aberdeen in Scotland discovered that it caused running fits in dogs. 'But dogs are not humans,' said the millers. Further investigations, however, showed that it also deranged the human mind.

The U. S. Government finally proscribed it. The millers have gone back to chlorine dioxide, once abandoned as dangerous, toxic and explosive.

A dough conditioner is now added, ammonium chloride, which has a simple poison rating of 3. Then polyoxyethylene is added, a softener. This is an intense skin irritant which has sickened rats and killed hamsters in experiments conducted by Dr. Edward Eagle, of Swift and Company, but it's not considered a serious poison. The softener is used because people like to squeeze the bread they buy, believing that if it's soft it's also fresh.[18]

An antioxidant, ditertiary-butyl-para-cresol, poison rating of 4, is added. To improve the gluten quality of the flour, a little bromate, toxicity rating of 5, is added. Bromate tends to destroy the kidneys and cause liver necrosis. Finally, calcium propionate is added, an antifungal compound to keep the bread from becoming moldy. This is commercial bread."

If all that isn't enough, we have heard that the fine, silky consistency of white flour comes from the talcum powder they add. True or not, the story of white flour and white bread is bad enough that we flatly refuse to eat it.

---

18. We personally know of a resort restaurant that had left-over hamburger buns at the end of their six-month season. They had been purchased at the beginning of the season and showed no signs of mold, dryness or staleness.

OILS

Cooking oils are said to be good for us, and we are recommended to have at least one tablespoonful per day. Let's learn something about them.

If the oil you have in your cupboard is bland, odorless, light-colored and clear, chances are it was over-processed and thus no longer has the healthful nutrients your body needs.

There are three methods of extracting vegetable oils from nuts, grains, beans, seeds or olives. The oldest and best method is cold-pressing, and it is accomplished by the use of an hydraulic press. However, there are only two materials that will yield enough oil by this method without first being heated: sesame seeds and olives. So only olive oil and sesame oil can ever legitimately be called "cold-pressed."

Another method of extracting oil is called "expeller pressed," and involves putting cooked material into one end of a screw or continuous press with a constantly rotating worm shaft. It continues under pressure until discharged at the other end with oil squeezed out. Since the temperatures are normally between 200 and 250 degrees, many nutrients have been destroyed. And what's more, expeller pressed oils generally are refined after extraction. The label to look for is "expeller-pressed-crude."

The third method is the one most commonly used by big commercial oil processors because it gets more oils out quickly and cheaply: oil-bearing materials are ground up, steam cooked, then mixed with a solvent of petroleum base which dissolves out the oils. The solvent is later separated from the oils. This is called solvent extraction. If the oxygen didn't destroy nutrients when the bean (or whatever) was ground, and the heat didn't destroy the nutrients, the use of the petroleum base solvent should be enough to prevent any health-minded person from using this type oil. The processors claim that only little, if any, solvent remains. Perhaps, but these solvents (the most common of them are types of naptha, pentane, heptane, hexane, and octane, and synthetic trichorethylene) can be harmful if any residue does remain. The International Union Against Cancer observed, "Since various petroleum constituents, including certain mineral oils and paraffin, have produced cancer in man and experimental animals, the presence of such chemicals in food appears to be objectionable, particularly when such materials are heated to high temperatures."

Once the oils are obtained, they are refined, usually with the addition of sodium hydroxide and temperatures around 450 degrees, and then with filtering, deodorizing, and bleaching. Such refining is an effort to get rid of impurities, like chlorophyll, vitamin A, vitamin E and phosphorous compounds such as lecithin.

Encyclopedia Britannica says of refined oils:

Refined oils are low in color, [thinner] and more susceptible to rancidity. [With bleaching] physical absorption methods involve treating hot oils with activated carbons, fullers earths or activated clays. Many impurities including chlorophyll and [vitamin A] are absorbed onto the agents and removed by filtration. Bleaching by any of these means reduces the resistance of oils to rancidity.

And of course, as with the refining of white flour, removal of nutrients, causes increased susceptibility to rancidity and makes it necessary to add preservatives.

In fact, the refining process is so perfect in obtaining an odor-free and flavor-free product, that rancid oil can be *reclaimed* and sold for human consumption. Whether this is actually happening or not, we don't know.

In buying oil, remember that there is no legal definition for the extraction and/or refining methods used. Unless you can find brands labeled by an organization called the Organic Merchants, then guide yourself by price (generally) and appearance. The blander, clearer, least flavorful are probably the most refined. Those with stronger, hearty color and fuller flavor will probably be the least refined, since the natural vitamins A and E, natural lecithin, and the other food factors Mother Nature included in the original bean or seed are what give the oil its color and flavor.

SALT

Salt is often blamed for creating or aggravating certain illnesses. Still, many of us, especially those with low blood sugar, are salt deficient. Aware that many health-minded people prefer no salt at all, we believe that salt can be a useful, tasteful and nutritional addition to a diet that is balanced, full-bodied, and healthy. A full, varied diet of properly prepared natural foods should keep the body free from the usual ailments.[19] And good salt can add important minerals to the healthy body.

Salt (sodium) with potassium stabilized the acid-base relationship in the body. We need sodium to maintain a normal balance of water between the cells and fluids to help nerves respond to stimulation, to help muscles contract, to aid in excretion of excess carbon dioxide. Sodium combines with chlorine to improve blood and lymph.

Lack of sodium produces such symptoms as headache, cramping, fatigue, heat stroke and retarded growth.

On the other hand, any amount of muscular activity saps the potassium in our bodies and sodium pours into the cells to fill the vacancy, changing the acid-alkaline balance, or pH, of the cell. This produces a toxic condition which in turn fosters the formation of dead tissue, which can block the arteries and is the prelude to sudden death from a heart attack.

A "good" salt is a sea salt, containing natural minerals that have not been refined or *purified* out. Of course, all salt is sea salt, the inland salt being left from seas that once covered the earth millions of years ago. However, some of the minerals have been leached out of this inland sea salt over the years.

The salt available in supermarkets is refined *pure* salt, 99.99 per cent sodium chloride. The refining eliminated its trace minerals, and its high concentration of sodium chloride gives it its very salty taste. It is the refining, which produces such concentration in a very tight molecular bond, that causes salt put on food after it is cooked to remain on top of the food. We have often noticed how food cooked with salt did not taste the same as food salted after the cooking was done. This isn't true, though, of sea salt. Food salted with sea salt will taste just like food cooked with it, since it will dissolve into the food very quickly, rather than just sit on top of the food like its city cousin does.

---

19. If, however, the body is run down at the beginning, more than food—prescribed supplements from a doctor—would have to be used to build the body to the point where the "everyday" complaints go away, and stay away.

The *Salt Story*[20] tells what the refining of salt entails.

In solution, salt is pumped up a long cylinder. Under great pressure, steam heat is applied to a temperature of 1,200 degrees Farenheit, running all the way up the length of the cylinder, causing the salt to crystallize instantly when the cylinder is 'flash-cooled.' This method saves money, but the salt crystal that comes out is very hard to digest. The crystal is extremely small, compared with the crystal that is formed in the sun-drying process. The molecular bond is tighter. When we eat this 'pure' small-crystal salt, we invariably increase our consumption of liquid. To prove this, please try these two simple experiments: First, place a teaspoonful of salt in an eight ounce glass of water and stir it once. Look at it several hours later. Is there any sediment? If so, the salt was refined; it isn't totally soluble, either in water or in our blood. Natural sea salt will seem to disappear in the water within a few minutes. Test number two is as follows: take a pinch of natural sea salt and place it on your tongue. Then do the same with refined commercial salt. Which one makes you more thirsty?

And with processing comes additives.

The first is potassium iodide in 'iodized' salt, to prevent goiter. Then, since iodine is very volatile and oxidizes in direct sunlight, dextrose, a simple sugar, is added to stabilize it. The third additive is sodium bicarbonate. This is needed to keep the salt looking white, as without it potassium iodide would make it turn purple. The fourth is sodium silico aluminate, or in some cases, magnesium carbonate. This coats each crystal and prevents the salt from attracting moisture.

Some people who prefer to avoid the use of any kind of salt use granulated sea kelp instead. (It comes in powdered form too, but has a much stronger flavor.) Powdered kelp has a

---

20. Erewhon, *The Salt Story* (Culver City, California: Erewhon).

somewhat fishy, sea-flavor and needs an acquired taste. We recommend that you buy granulated kelp using it on nearly all your foods. We season our food at the table, or mix it with sea salt. It can be used wherever you presently use salt.

Another good seasoning is sea salt mixed with roasted sesame seeds. (Recipe is in this book.)

Confessions of a Sneaky Organic Cook, recommends easy ways to do without salt.[21] In place of salt they recommend going creative with all kinds of herbs—dill, oregano, rosemary, thyme, basil, caraway, sesame and poppy seeds, for instance: chives on eggs, basil on tomatoes, rosemary on lamb, or nutmeg on broccoli. Bay leaves and onions on roasting meats is not only a good substitute, but a delicious added flavor.

Since we are introducing our readers to health foods, we want them to taste as much like usual as possible. We use sea salt in our recipes. You won't notice any difference in flavor.

But you are aware now of the possible dangers of using too much salt, and you will probably want to decrease its use whenever you can. We have found that whole living foods, cooked as we describe, don't lose their nutrients and flavor into the air or water and therefore need very little seasoning. Also, salting with sea salt after cooking, just the top of the food means that the first bites taste salty, and all the rest after them seem salty.

PRESERVATIVES AND OTHER ADDITIVES

We recommend eating nothing with preservatives or additives of any kind. For the most part they consist of chemical substances that are either directly harmful poisons to the body, or which are unassimilated by the body, accumulating in areas like the colon, until they become an irritant and produce a stress situation, providing the environment for disease to take hold.

Nearly all the foods found in supermarkets contain these products of modern chemistry, and one of the most harmful and widespread is the nitrate-nitrite additive. We treat both additives the same, since nitrates break down into nitrites by microbial action either prior to ingestion or within the gastro-

---

21. Hypoglycemics are usually deficient in salt and will probably not want to limit their intake.

intestinal tract. This reduction produces the symptoms of nitrate toxicity. Both nitrate and nitrite freely traverse the gastro-intestinal wall into the blood stream where nitrite oxidized the ferrous iron of the red blood pigment hemoglobin and causes a reduced availability of oxygen to the tissues. In simpler language the nitrates decrease the bloods ability to carry oxygen, resulting in increasing incidence of respiratory failure.

Further, nitrate can interfere with normal iodine metabolism of the thyroid gland and cause a reduction in the storage of vitamin A by the liver. Nitrate in any quantity makes it impossible for our bodies to convert carotene (from carrots and other vegetables) into usable vitamin A, which is an infection-fighting vitamin.

There is also a relationship between nitrates and sexual performance. Nutritionist Jane Kinderlehrer recommends not serving hot dogs if you're in the mood for a night of love.

Frankfurters and all preserved meats are loaded with nitrates and nitrites. And what nitrates and nitrites do to sexuality, you will comprehend better when you realize that another name for potassium nitrate is saltpeter, the substance that was, at one time, sprinkled on the food of prisoners in order to stifle sexual desire.[22]

The next question is, why are nitrates and nitrites used? In the case of farming, high nitrogen fertilizers are used to improve crop production. It appears that while production goes up, quality of the food decreases. In general, heavy applications of nitrogen will decrease the calcium and phosphorus content of plants.[23]

To make things worse, the run-off water from such fields tends to flow into lakes and rivers, increasing the nitrate content of the water used for drinking and raising other edible plants.

Nitrates are also widely used in preserving food. They are frequently added to packaged foods for preservation, and

---

22. Jane Kinderlehrer, *Confessions of a Sneaky Organic Cook*, p. 86.
23. *Basic Book of Organically Grown Foods* (Emmaus, Pa.: Rodale Press).

sausages, cured and canned meats, fish and pickled meats are treated with both sodium nitrate and nitrite. Meats get their red color and look fresher than they are from the nitrates, which also preserve the pink color of cured meats (which, besides the sugar used in curing, is why we recommend not eating commercially-cured meats like ham). In baby foods, nitrates make for a longer shelf life.

Many foods in the supermarket contain additives that are not listed on the labels (the FDA is inconsistent, to put it mildly) and we normally wouldn't suspect that they are there.[24] One of these is carageenan, beneficial in its natural form. But this seaweed is now bleached with sulfer dioxide, cleaned with alkali and treated with charcoal and alcohol, according to Beatrice Trumm Hunter in her article in *Consumer Bulletin,* May, 1972. It has been incriminated in causing such disturbances in animals as ulcerative colitis, and when injected into rats malignant tumors have formed at the site of the injection.

Linda Clarke says that carageenan is added:

> . . . not only to cottage cheese, but to canned milk and many other foods to provide 'body' and smoothness. It is used in commercial gelatin desserts, baked goods, candies, canned meats and pet foods, baby foods, yogurt, cheese, ice creams, and milk drinks as well as to clarify juices, vinegar, wines and beer to control beer foam. It is also used in toothpastes, hand lotions, deodorants, spermatocidal jellies and pharmaceuticals.[25]

It is because the diabetic and dietetic foods contain chemical preservatives as well as coal tar based sweeteners

---

25. Linda Clarke, *Let's Live* (September, 1972).

24. It is important to remember this. What you read is not always all you get. Many ingredients are simply not required to be listed on labels, and some items are grouped together under one generic name. Unless it says, e. g., "No Preservatives," the item you are considering may have preservatives. And even when some preservatives or additives are named, there may be some that are not listed.

that we oppose them. Besides, since they are processed, they have lost about 30 per cent of their food value.

With respect to chemical additives, Dr. U. Coda Martin, president of the American Academy of Nutrition, points out that the human body can utilize only natural food as nourishment and survive. If we accept this premise, then since chemicals aren't food elements they can produce only negative or harmful results, even those scientifically classified as non-toxic. The only question is how much harm they will do when used in place of essential food elements in our diets.

Section III
Getting Down
to the Basics

Section III

GETTING DOWN
TO THE BASICS

PROTEIN

Protein in our diets is absolutely essential, yet most of us have very little knowledge of how to obtain it, other than from meat and dairy products. Protein starvation is not uncommon among young people who become vegetarians without studying nutrition.

Protein contains nitrogen, sulfur and phosphorus, which are essential to life. The body's framework is made up of protein just as the framework of a plant is cellulose. Hormones, which regulate metabolic processes of the body are protein, as are the catalysts of these processes, enzymes. Hemoglobin, the part of blood which carries oxygen, is protein. Protein in the blood maintains the pH balance of the blood and maintains the water balance between cell walls. (We've all seen pictures of starving children with distended bellies—the protein deficiency has allowed water fluids to build up in the interstitial tissues between the cells.) Protein is needed for antibody formation to fight infection.

Unlike many other substances, we can't store protein, and the amino acids that make up the protein family can be depleted in a couple of hours, and even more rapidly under stress situations. In fact, during periods of stress we consume large quantities of liquid protein.

When someone says protein, most of us think of meat or milk. But vegetable protein is good, readily available, and generally cheaper. In fact, many people prefer not to eat meat at all since (1) meat tends to be mucous-forming in the body, decreasing the body's ability to cleanse itself and fight off illness, since (2) much of the commercial meat has been fed female hormones while alive, considered by many to be cancer-producing[1], and since (3) meat, being high on the food chain, is more likely to contain accumulated contaminates from the environment, and since (4) meat often carries with it worms and/or disease.

But the very fact that meat is expensive is enough reason for us to look at other sources of protein for our diet.

First, let's clarify what we mean when we talk about protein value. Generally nutritionists, dieters and doctors simply look at the list of foods whose protein value is measured by grams per weight. This is misleading because the protein group contains 22 amino acids, eight of them unable to be synthesized by our bodies. For this reason these eight are called Essential Amino Acids (EAAs), and include tryptophan, leucine, isoleucine, lysine, valine, threonine, the sulfur-containing amino acids, and the aromatic amino acids.

For these amino acids to be used by the body, they must all be present at the same time, and in the right proportions. Frances Moore Lappe explains;

> *If you eat protein containing enough tryptophan to satisfy 100 per cent of the utilizable pattern's requirement, 100 per cent of the leucine level and so forth, but only 50 per cent of the necessary lysine, then, as far as your body is concerned, you might as well have eaten only 50 per cent of ALL the EAAs. Only 50 per cent of the protein you ate is used as protein and the rest is literally wasted. The protein 'assembling center' in the cell uses the EAAs at the level of the 'limiting amino acid' and releases the left-over amino acids to be used by the body as fuel as if they were lowly carbohydrates.*[2]

Miss Lappe goes on to measure all proteins according to their NPU—Net Protein Utilization, and this brings surprising results. In grams of protein per weight, milk and eggs rate low,

---

1. *Laetrile—a Control for Cancer* (New York: Warner Books Inc.).

2. Frances M. Lappe, *Diet for a Small Planet* (New York: Ballantine, 1971) pp. 30, 31.

while meat rates high. But in terms of usable protein, eggs rate the highest on the chart, with milk next, and meat ranks down with soybeans, whole rice, wheat germ, rice germ, oatmeal, and buckwheat (all in their natural, unprocessed form, of course).

Thus we see that while the proportions of amino acids in animal meat correspond more closely to our body requirements than do the amino acid proportions of vegetable protein, nevertheless we could survive quite well with vegetable protein. We could eat more quantity of the vegetable to get more protein, or mix it with eggs and dairy products: or, and this is Lappe's creative and useful suggestion, eat a variety of plant proteins that have complementary amino acid patterns.

In her book you will find charts showing the NPU of various foods, and rating the availability of the EEAs for each food. By finding that one food is poor is lysine, for example, we search through the charts to find one that is high in lysine, and then eat the two foods together. For example, rice and beans are complementary, wheat and cheese, rice and sesame seeds, corn and beans, and so on. And if meat is used as a complement, only very small portions need be used. Turkey has the best NPU rating of meats, and used with one part to five parts of wheat or black-eyed peas will give you more protein than an entire meal of beef.

What we are talking about is a situation where the whole is greater than the sum of the individual foods used. Not only is this important to low-blood sugar sufferers, but to budget-minded families as well. This way you can get the most out of your food dollar.

Here is a first-hand example of how well this works. Being hypoglycemic, we usually have to snack at least 2 hours after our meals, when hunger pangs or shaking hands warn us that our blood sugar has dropped too far. Recently, testing the theory, we added cheese to our breakfast of whole wheat French toast. The egg is complete enough in itself, but the wheat bread lacked some EAAs. The cheese filled in the EAAs that the wheat lacked, and we have no signs of low blood sugar hunger pangs for more than four hours after breakfast. (When we used bread that was not 100 per cent whole wheat, the results decreased.) Nothing else was done differently in the food preparation. A tiny piece of cheese made the difference. While we still did not have a perfect protein, it was very satisfactory, and we were pleasantly surprised.

As for other nutrients contained in meat, only one, cobalamin (Vitamin B-12) is lacking in plant protein. But since this can readily be obtained through eggs and dairy products, there is no problem for a person wanting to avoid meat and obtain all the necessary protein and nutrients through plants, supplemented by eggs and dairy products.

Another interesting finding of Miss Lappe is that gelatin, so often prescribed to us because of its supposed protein value, has a Net Protein Utilization of only 2, and what's more it can reduce the usability of other protein eaten with it.

We recommend her book for an in-depth understanding of her thesis. It includes charts of food groups, indicating the NPU and EAA strength of each food, as well as menus and recipes, and best protein buys and best protein sources calorie-wise.

PREPARATION TIME
AND NATURAL FOOD COOKING

One argument against eating natural foods is that too much time would be spent cooking. It is true that a little extra time is spent, though not much , in the kitchen. When you're first learning, sometimes you can't find any of those strange foods that the recipe calls for that you KNOW you just bought at the store. When you got home you removed them from their sacks and put them into containers, and now you can't remember which container holds what. This does take time, but it's only the time of getting organized.

The time you will notice the difference is when you come home late and have to fix a quick meal, and there are no cans or boxes to open. Usually this can be taken care of by having some chili beans or cooked rice left-overs in the refrigerator. Chili beans, salad and corn bread, or salad and fried rice with sesame seeds and nuts are quick and nutritious, high-protein meals. So is fish (not the breaded kind) and omelets and egg sandwiches made with melted cheese and sprouts.

Frances Lappe timed herself to see if she really spent more time cooking this way.

You may be feeling that cooking in this new way will require too much of your time. After all there are no prepackaged, instant complementary protein combinations on the grocery shelf! I used to resist making even so-called 'quick' breads from scratch. How could they be as quick as a ready-made mix? But I began to want to make dishes that demanded I start from scratch. I decided to test myself. How much more time did it actually take to make my cornbread recipe than a commercial cornbread mix? I was surprised to find that it hardly took any more time at all! Both required that I get out bowls and utensils, and then the baking pan. The only difference was that for my recipe I had to combine a few more ingredients—a really minor part of the whole operation.[3]

We feel that the rewards in better health are worth a little extra time.

HEALTH FOOD COSTS SO MUCH!

NOT TRUE! The reason is that whole food goes farther. Money isn't going to processers and chemists and Madison Avenue, but into the food. It is true that, for example, a package of whole wheat spaghetti costs more per package than a package of the pasty, white type, but a smaller helping of wheat spaghetti will satisfy your hunger and you won't have to eat as much. While the obvious cost per item is higher, you spend less because you eat less.

Also, we have many misconceptions about what are cheap foods and what are costly foods. Lappe did an analysis and found, to her surprise and ours, that tuna actually costs more than swordfish, and only 14 cents per pound less than canned salmon, while crab costs only slightly more than peanuts.

Sometime count up the money you spent on the non-food items in your pantry—crackers made with white flour and sugar, cookies, potato chips and tortilla chips, soda pop, and so on. That is all wasted money as far as food value is concerned. And that's not mentioning the questionable food values of such things as sandwich bologna, breakfast drinks, and imitation dairy products, to mention a few. What we need to consider is the actual food value of each item in relation to its cost.

---

3. Frances M. Lappe, *Diet for a Small Planet* (New York: Ballantine, 1971), p. 128.

Another advantage in using natural foods is that in most cases you can buy the basics in bulk—the grains like rice, wheat, triticali, and legumes like corn, black-eyed peas, black beans, split peas, seeds, nuts, flours, and juices.

We know of families living on a couple of thousand dollars a year who eat very well on so-called health foods. As we see it, cost is not a legitimate excuse for failing to eat natural foods. It's a cop-out.

WEIGHT CONTROL

"But," you argue, "I could never have a meal of chili beans, corn spoon bread and salad. Why, I'd gain weight in a minute."

All we can say is that we haven't, and don't believe you will, unless it is improperly prepared and doesn't follow the guidelines of balance. If you are seriously underweight, we'll wager that you will gain weight up to your normal level, and then you will maintain that weight. A noted nutritionist, pointing out that 9 out of 10 of the nation's overweight are suffering with hypoglycemia, commented that by adhering to the principles of the hypoglycemic diet, which is essentially what we offer in this book, the whole family will benefit, whether they are fatties or twiggies, because the diet is based on sound nutrition principles that tend to normalize the weight.

Your two authors had problems both ways. One constantly had to count calories (though it didn't seem so to her friends), while the other was grossly underweight. On this diet, one lost and one gained, to where we both obtained and maintained a normal weight. And this was accomplished in spite of having to snack almost continually throughout the day, and even during the night.

This program includes no processed carbohydrates, which are essentially high-calorie non-foods that turn into fat and raise the blood sugar level quickly, which results in a rapid fall of sugar in the blood—the initiator of hunger pangs. Rather we emphasize sufficient protein, which, while it too is converted into glycogen by the body, it is converted slowly, so that the blood sugar maintains a constant level over a long period of time. Calorie for calorie, protein *sticks* with us longer than will sugar or carbohydrate, preventing sudden drops in the sugar level of the blood which in turn causes us to feel hungry and eat. In short, this *diet* represents a balance of the food nutrients we need, so that what we eat will be utilized by the body, not just stored as fat. The food will become energy, disease-fighters and body-builders.

We eat until we are physically satisfied. We believe that if you live the concept of balance in your diet, chances are good that you won't become overweight. If, however, you eat a whole meal of beans, because you love beans and we say they are good, and you don't also have cheese and/or corn and/or rice with them, as well as a salad or vegetable, then you will gain weight because you have ignored balance. We can't emphasize enough the importance of balance. Also, during times of inactivity we don't require as much food, and if we overeat then, it is through psychological habit, and not physical need, and we will gain weight because we have again ignored balance—in this case the balance of need and intake.

PROPER COOKING METHODS

We have been talking about proper food preparation. Here is what we mean.

Food must not be heated above 180 degrees. Heat higher than 180 degrees destroys vital food elements. Even at that temperature, some enzymes are destroyed. For example a potato is a good source of protein as well as thiamine (B-1), riboflavin (B-2), niacin, Vitamin C, iron, and potassium when low-heat cooked in no water and left with the peeling intact. Peeling the potato cuts away the belt of minerals lying just under the skin. And if the heat is so hot that you can't hold your hand comfortably over the open pan (which is uncovered just long enough for the test), then the protein is being chemically changed. It is converted into substances that no longer act in the body with the same chemical properties of the original protein.

Here are some guidelines to follow. Re-train yourself to turn the stove on to medium rather than high, and as soon as the food is warm, or the water is simmering (give it the hand-above test), turn the heat way back, keeping the pan covered, and let the low heat do the cooking. In good stainless cookware it won't take any longer than it did at high temperatures, and it won't require water.

Some stoves are quite hot even on the lowest setting, in which case the heat must be turned off completely or the pan can be moved slightly off the burner, or, preferably, make yourself a butterfly-shaped wire rack from an old coat hanger, and put it on top of the burner and under the pan when your turn back the heat.

Other robbers of food nutrients are the paring knife, water, and air. Don't peel, unless you absolutely have to, and then save the peelings for your stock. Using water to cook should become a thing of the past. Stock can be used for gravies and cooking rice and beans and such, and frozen vegetables need no water added at all. When they are cooked you will pour off more than ½ cup of water, produced, we assume, by the process of freezing. Only in some chicken dishes might you use water rather than stock (unless you have homemade chicken stock), since most vegetable stock is strong and will overwhelm the delicate flavor of chicken. Of course, steaming vegetables requires water, which the food never touches. And this water is saved for the stock jar.

Be careful when washing your food. Don't let it soak in water, and wash it quickly. Important vitamins and minerals which are water soluble can be lost in the water at this stage, too. This means that you no longer soak cucumbers, onions, radishes or carrots in water to make them crisp and milder.

Keep food covered at all times. Many nutrients, like Vitamins E and C, oxidize readily when they come in contact with the air. This means covering not only all food as it is cooking (except for frying) but covering left-overs and half-eaten apples and unused lemon wedges and so on.

To cook waterless and with low heat it is best to have very good, heavy stainless steel cookware. Good stainless is one of the best investments in health a person can make, if he will use it properly. There is one brand that has a flipper gauge in the lids to tell the cook when to turn down the heat before the food reaches 180 degrees.[4]

But if you don't have stainless cookware, and can't get it, you can still cook properly, though it will take a little longer. Use glass, porcelain or pottery. Pans in any case should be heavy, with tight-fitting lids. Cook with as little water as your pans will allow, and what water you do use and is left over when you are done should be added to the stock jar. It will be full of the nutrients you lost from your food, and the sink doesn't need them, but you do. Never waste them.

By no means cook in aluminum or teflon. Teflon scratches down to the aluminum underneath, and also gives off fluorine

---

4. For information, write: *Saladmaster of Utah*
                      P. O. Box 20401
                      Granger, Utah 84120.

gas when it reaches a certain temperature. Because aluminum is porous (and teflon is covering aluminum), hot food gets into the metal pores, and when the pan cools slightly before it is washed the pores contract and close, trapping the food particles inside. When the pan is heated again, those pores will open and the food from the last meal will come out into the food presently being cooked in them. Not a very sanitary thought. Iron is also porous and works the same way, only more so. According to studies done by the U. S. government, materials used in cookware and rated according to food retention ranged from 0.00 for heavy-gauge stainless teeel and glass to very high for cast iron. Aluminum was in the middle.

Inexpensive stainless steamers are available in most department stores, discount stores, variety stores, health food stores and specialty gift catalogues. They fit inside whatever pans you presently have. We suggest getting at least two so you can steam both potatoes and vegetables for the same meal. (We always steam rather than simmer our potatoes.) Or you can make a steamer from a porcelain double boiler by punching holes with a hot ice pick into the bottom of the top pan.

Since the key to healthy eating is balance, every care must be taken not to destroy any of the natural food components. High heat, water, cutting, peeling, and air can destroy food quality and leave you with nutritionally worthless food.

HEALTH FOOD STORES

The first time I walked into a health food store I was excited, confused, and totally bewildered. It was a world I had no knowledge of and I ended up buying some powdered protein and vitamin C tablets, and I left.

We have watched women walk into natural food stores, their eyes full of excitement and anticipation. They look at the products with wonder—"I wonder what it's for? How does it taste? How do I fix it? Why would I eat it in the first place?"

Some of our readers may have already been introduced to health food outlets, but for those of you who have never been in one, let us take you on a tour.

Not all health food stores carry the products you'll want to use. Some carry primarily supplements in powdered and tablet form. These include vitamins and minerals, wheat germ and wheat germ oil, food yeast and bone meal, cayenne, kelp, calcium and protein powder, to mention a few of them.

Some stores specialize in untreated whole grains, cereals and legumes, like wheat, triticali (a cross between wheat and rye), rye, buckwheat, millet, barley, oatmeal, split peas, lentils, etc. They will probably also carry raw nuts and seeds, usually shelled and hulled, as well as dried fruits (dried without preservatives or chemicals).

Other stores will carry dairy products such as raw milk, yogurts and cheeses from goat as well as cow milk, and unadulterated ice cream sweetened with honey. Usually available through these grocery-like stores are organically grown vegetables and fruits, and cold-pressed oils, as well as raw honey.

Most of the stores will carry the natural sweeteners like raw honey, unsulphured molasses, sorghum, and occasionally, date sugar, as well as an assortment of herbal teas, natural, unsweetened fruit juices (and some raw fresh vegetable juices like carrot juice), grain products like whole wheat spaghetti and barley macaroni, organic rice and sesame chips (like T.V. snack chips). They will probably also carry good quality cider vinegar, mayonnaise with no sugar, preservatives or chemical additives, and low-sodium baking powder.

Most natural food stores carry an assortment of books on both foods and natural remedies, plus the latest editions of such magazines as *Let's Live, Prevention,* and *Organic Gardening.*

As you can see, you probably won't be able to do all your shopping in one place.

BASICS

The following items are used in recipes in this book. If you plan to use the menus, we suggest you go shopping first.

WHEAT GERM: both raw and toasted.

WHEAT GERM OIL: Many people believe wheat germ oil is absolutely essential to good health. Others claim that the second air and light hit the oil it oxidizes and loses its beneficial qualities.

SEEDS: raw and hulled. Again, some claim they should not be hulled because of loss of nutrients upon exposure to air, but if you're going to get into the habit of using them, they'd best be handy, and it isn't handy to hull seeds. We especially recommend pumpkin seeds, sesame seeds, and sunflower seeds. For starters, use the sesame seeds for breading and filler where you once used bread crumbs, and they're good ground and added to sauces and gravies. Use pumpkin seeds on the peanut butter sandwiches, and the sunflower seeds on all your salads for an added crunchiness.

NUTS: These should also be raw, and while they are good for us, some contain a very high fat content per unit of usable protein, so eaten in quantity they would tend to be fattening. This is true of almonds, pecans, walnuts, and especially the English walnuts. We recommend cashews, whose NPU matches sunflower seeds, making it equal to the seeds in their protein quality. (Most nuts rate lower than seeds in NPU.)

UNSWEETENED COCONUT: This is good for frostings, with raw honey and nuts, and we always add it to our homemade granola. Coconut is not terribly low in natural carbohydrate content, and in sufficient amounts will probably produce a reaction in a hypoglycemic.

WHOLE GRAIN FLOURS: Our recipes call for whole wheat, soy, and triticali flours. While we don't include recipes using rice flour, rye flour, barley or buckwheat flour, you may want to buy some and experiment. There are many good recipes available using these different flours.

CORN MEAL: Buy 100 per cent fresh ground corn meal. Some natural food stores will grind their own right there in the store.

LEGUMES: You will want to stock up on black-eyed peas, pinto beans, split peas, and black turtle beans. Soy beans also are very high in NPU and considered an excellent meat substitute. They have a fairly strong flavor and might take some getting used to. They can be mixed with other beans, like pinto beans, and made into a chili bean dish. There is a cookbook available that specializes in soy recipes, called *The Soybean Cookbook* (Arco Publishing Co., 219 Park Avenue South, New York, New York, 10003).

SEA SALT: See salt section.

LOW SODIUM BAKING POWDER: There are different brands available. After reading about salt, you know why we prefer the low-sodium baking powder. We never use baking soda. In recipes using soda, just add more baking powder, or leave it out altogether. Some people substitute with food yeast.

BONE MEAL: See page 67.

RAW HONEY: Unprocessed honey still has all the good vitamins and enzymes that nature and the bees put into it. This includes the B vitamins needed for digestion of the honey as well as some trace minerals and the natural enzymes credited by some for helping fight the effects of asthma and hayfever. It is a wholesome food, a purifying cleanser for the body, and has been said to have rejuvenating powers.

ONIONS: A good natural source of vitamin C.

GARLIC: An equally good source of vitamin C, and, like onions, a good seasoning. The most flavor is obtained from the garlic by pressing the clove in a garlic press, usually sold in the kitchen section of department and appliance stores.

DRY SEASONING: Here we include garlic powder, granulated onion, Vegesal, and Spike. Be sure to read the labels. Many seasonings, especially those found in the supermarkets, contain sugar, and preservatives,. It is usually safe to buy the seasonings in health food stores.

CAYENNE: According to herbal books, cayenne is more than just a seasoning. It is a fantastic, nutritious food as well as a body cleanser. Among other things it is claimed that cayenne, taken regularly, will help to regulate blood pressure, build resistance to infectious diseases, aid digestion, heal ulcers, and stop hemorrhaging.

CIDER VINEGAR: A good vinegar will cost around three times more than the supermarket variety. It is also stronger, but contains none of the chemical acids used to ferment the usual supermarket brands. Two good brands to buy are Sterling and Healthwise.

CAROB: Carob, also called St. John's Bread, is a chocolate substitute and a rich food, containing important vitamins and minerals, including a proper balance of calcium, iron, magnesium, phosphorus, and potassium. Be sure you buy the toasted kind, since the raw carob does not taste at all like chocolate. It can be purchased as a candy or a powder, for use in hot drinks, flavoring, cooking, and baking. Carob chips are also available, but usually contain raw sugar. The carob bean comes from an evergreen tree and is believed to be what St. John lived on during his sojourn in the wilderness. Thus it has been called St. John's bread. It is also said that the beans are the original carat weight of goldsmiths.

Carob is low in calories, high in natural sugars, contains the B-complex vitamins and vitamin A, and it is a reservoir of minerals. Unlike chocolate it won't kick up allergies or cause tooth decay. It is a legume of low allergenic potential. According to the FDA's Composition of Foods, 100 grams of carob powder yields only 180 calories, only 1.4 grams of fat, and supplies 80.7 grams of total carbohydrate, of which 7.7

grams are roughage (thus it has been used to counteract diarrhea, especially in children and infants). The B-vitamins help soothe the digestive tract back to normal.

Carob contains other health factors. Since it is rich in pectin, a valuable aid in controlling cholesterol levels, carob has marked mechanical and detoxifying properties. In a mechanical way it absorbs toxins and bacteria formed in the intestinal tract, and inhibits their formation. It further acts as a buffer.

Carob satisfies the sweet tooth, provides energy, tastes a lot like chocolate, and is a healthy, nutritious, low-calorie food.

SPROUTING SEEDS: Alfalfa, wheat and mung are the most commonly sprouted seeds, though you may want to try oats, soy, and rye as well.

RAW MILK: Raw milk still contains its natural lecithin, since no high heat has been used to process it. It not only contains this natural cholesterol fighter, but it is easier to digest than pasteurized milk, and does not taste any different.

GOAT CHEESE: This is a good substitute for sour cream, as is goat yogurt. Try it on top of sweetened, fresh strawberries.

FERTILE EGGS: These eggs contain hormones that non-fertile eggs don't have even a trace of. Second-best are eggs from chickens allowed to scratch and peck in the barnyard.

MOLASSES: This comes from the bottom of the barrel, so to speak, in the sugar refining process. It is there that the vitamins and minerals go, including vitamin K and the B vitamins. In fact, it contains all the components—B vitamins, copper, and iron, used in natural re-coloring of animal furs. (Take note, grey-haired readers.) Blackstrap molasses is the strongest in flavor, and the highest in nutrients. Add only a dash to anything you want flavored like brown sugar. (After all, that is how they make commercial brown sugar.) Add it to your diet gradually, since it is a powerful laxative.

SORGHUM: The first extraction from the sugar cane, it is a mild-flavored sweetener excellent for baking and cooking as well as for topping spoon bread, pancakes, and the like. Read the label and choose a brand that has been extracted from organically grown cane, without the use of excess high heat. Severely hypoglycemic people may not be able to tolerate sorghum at first.

SOY SAUCE: Preferably buy a brand like Tamari, which has been naturally fermented, with no sugar added.

PEANUT BUTTER: This should be purchased raw, or sun-roasted. Raw nut butters taste quite a bit different from what we are used to. Some people really like them, especially the raw cashew butter. We prefer the sun-roasted type made from peanuts that were first roasted in the sun. One brand is the *Deaf Smith* peanut butter. You can also make your own. Grind peanuts in the blender, and add just enough oil to make them spreadable. If the peanuts are raw, the flavor will resemble fresh green garden peas.

PROTEIN POWDER: Should contain the least amount of carbohydrate possible, and should not contain any sugar. Read the label carefully. Two excellent brands, although there are others, are Protesoy, and the Neo-life company's Super Ease. These two dissolve very well in juice and milk.

MAYONNAISE: Found in supermarkets generally contains sugar, cornstarch and food starch. Find a brand that doesn't contain these. Of course, your best bet is the natural food stores, but read the label anyway. There is even dairyless mayonnaise available for those who have low tolerance to milk and dairy products, or who otherwise wish to avoid eggs.

SORBITOL: A fruit sugar coming primarily from France. It is sweeter than refined sugar, and often recommended by doctors for diabetics, since some believe it is sucrose rather than this fructose that causes problems. However, Dr. Carleton Frederick points to studies done by Dr. John Yudkin that cite the opposite: that the impact of sugar on the body is entirely different from that of starch; that starch is innocent of producing the *coronary profile;* that starch converts into glucose and fructose; that since glucose is innocent of promoting heart and atherosclerosis problems, then the villain must be fructose. Dr. Yudkin says that "anything sucrose does, fructose does faster and in greater degree."[5] We do not recommend the use of sorbitol.

AGAR-AGAR: Is a natural thickener for fruits. It can be bought in powdered form in health food stores.

ARROWROOT: is a natural thickener for gravies, as a flour substitute. Use slightly more arrowroot than you would use flour. It comes in powdered form in most health food stores. (Whole wheat flour is a strong enough flavor that it often overwhelms the gravies or sauces. We use only arrowroot.)

---

5. *Prevention* (February, 1974), p. 70.

SEEDS

Seeds are the essence of life. Sprouted, they produce in abundance all the life-giving elements (See *Sprouting*). They contain fats, carbohydrates (in very low quantities), calcium, iron, phosphorus, potassium and other minerals as well as protein that they are capable of developing into complete patterns to sustain life.

All seeds are splendid food. Pumpkin seeds are recommended for fertility and keeping that sexual spark alive, since they contain zinc, a trace element important to virility and absent in most processed foods. Zinc is found in the bran and germ portions of cereal grains, and those very portions are removed in the refining process.

The prize seed is the sunflower seed. They are good for cheering you up, for raising the blood sugar during that mid-afternoon slump, for an energy pick-up, and they are said to be good for the eyes. The list of their benefits is too long to mention here, but there are a number of good books that will tell you about them.

Seeds can be sprouted and used in salads, dressing and such, or can be ground and used along with other flours for pancakes and waffles. Pumpkin seeds are good on top of peanut butter sandwiches, and sunflower seeds add a delicious crunchiness to green salads.

WHEAT GERM

Wheat germ the life-giving and life-sustaining part of wheat (which Is removed in processing) is a superior food. It contains protein, minerals, B vitamins, fat and carbohydrates in the right proportion for use by our bodies. As a protein it has a NPU factor of 67. That means that 67 per cent is utilized, which is high; and, it is high in lysine, which most nuts, seeds, grains, cereals, and flours (except wheat) are low in. It should always be added to these as a complementary protein.

Especially important is its vitamin E content, which is the major nutritional factor in wheat germ oil. Vitamin E is proving to be excellent for heart problems. In tests where cattle were deprived of wheat germ and Vitamin E they have dropped dead of heart disease. When the wheat germ-vitamin E was restored to their feed, the deaths from heart disease ceased. That is something! Unless you are taking wheat germ and oil supplements, and/or using whole grain bread (without additives) you aren't getting vitamin E. Processed foods eliminate it in the processing.

Raw wheat germ can be used wherever you formerly used bread crumbs or cracker crumbs: breading, batter, stuffing, filler for meat loaf and stuffed peppers, and it can be added to cereals, breads, muffins, and pancakes. It has a nutty rich taste and will not be unsavory to anyone. The nugget-like crunchy style germ has been roasted and is good in place of nuts on top of breads, cereals, and yogurt sundaes.

NUTRITIONAL YEAST
(Also called Brewer's Yeast and Food Yeast)

Brewer's yeast used to be an exclusive by-product of beer, but it has become so popular as a food that it is now made specifically as a food called nutritional or food yeast. It contains all the major B vitamins except B-12, which makes it a good nerve food. It contains 19 amino acids, making it a complete protein, and it contains at least 18 minerals.

Nutritional yeast comes in powder form and in large and small flakes. The flakes are milder in flavor, but you need to take more of them to get the same equivalent as the powder. The same is true of the tablets.

Besides being a nerve food and a reducing food, it is especially good as an energy food. A tablespoon or so added to some liquid will pick you up and hold you there for several hours. We know one woman who consumed large quantities of it, with very little additional food, for the year she was establishing her private school. She had no time for relaxation or diversion, and her life was one of little sleep, no regular home routine, and plenty of stress and anxiety. But every hour or so, as duties permitted, she would drink some yeast, and it kept her going. To our knowledge she didn't have a sick day that year.

Nutritional yeast is one of the best sources of niacin. Niacin deficiency is often found to be the cause of psychiatric disturbances. It has been used successfully in the treatment of schizophrenia. Lesser deficiencies can show themselves as depression, gloom, and Monday blues, dizziness, fatigue, backache, and melancholy.[6]

---

6. We were struck by the description from one of our returned Vietnam POW's who suffered severe burning pain, especially in his legs, while he was a prisoner. It was a B-

The key to health is balance, and certain minerals must be balanced together to work properly. This is true of phosphorus and calcium. Food yeast is high in phosphorus so calcium should be added to it. We buy powdered calcium lactate and add it to the yeast, ¼ cup calcium to one pound yeast. That way it is always ready for us to use.

Besides adding the yeast to liquids you can also use it wherever you use flour, as in gravies, stews, breads, rolls, batters, and breadings, but do so sparingly until a taste is developed for it. It has a *healthy* flavor, and if you introduce it all at once you may not like it, and may lose your interest in being willing to develop a taste for it. On the other hand, some people love the taste right off, and eat it undiluted.

A mild-flavored yeast called *fragilis* is available, and the information we have received on it is that it has all the food value of nutritional yeast, and possibly, even more.

BONE MEAL

Centuries ago our ancestor ate the bones of the animals they killed for food. Western Africans, who devour the bones along with the meat of their kills, have such strong teeth that they use them to open beer bottles.[7] If dogs don't eat bones, or get some bone meal in their food, they become weak and sick, and finally die from calcium deficiency.

While most of us don't have strong enough teeth to chew bones (since we have never done so to develop strong teeth), we can still get the benefits they offer from bone meal, available in health food stores. This meal is sterilized, pulverized long bones of calves, and is the answer to calcium nutrition. It contains twice as much calcium as phosphorus, which is helpful in balancing the dietary ratio of these minerals. The calcium present in the bones and bone meal helps in the utilization of the phosphorus. Bone meal also contains beneficial trace minerals, and all these nutrients are natural.

---

vitamin deficiency starving the nerves. It could have been partially helped by eating brown rice. We wonder how much B-vitamin the doctors gave him when he got home, and what kind of food he's eating now.

7. Cyril Maxton, "Are You Eating Your Way Into a Cast?" *Prevention* (April, 1973).

Bone meal can be added to gravies, breads, and mashed potatoes, and put into *shakes.* It is a good idea to taste it first, and then determine where you can sneak it into foods without its being noticed.

Or buy bone meal tablets and take them as supplements. Another method of obtaining the calcium from bones comes from Adele Davis:

You can increase the nutritive value of meats containing bone by soaking or cooking them with a little acid, as tomatoes, vinegar or sour cream. The acid dissolves some of the calcium from the bones into the gravy or sauce. If the cut does not contain bones, purchase bone to cook with any meat to be braised or stewed. A single serving of pickled pig's feet has been found to supply as much calcium as 3 quarts of milk.[8]

LECITHIN

Pronounced LESS-I-THIN, lecithin is found in every cell of the body, including the brain, and needs to remain there. It emulsifies cholesterol, distributes the body weight more evenly, aids heart disturbances (myasthenia gravis and agina), and appears to be helpful in preventing gallstones. It is found in the myelin sheath surrounding the nerves (and is therefore a natural tranquilizer) and is very necessary for the male sex glands, since lecithin is lost with the sperm.

Lecithin is made from soybeans and is available in liquid, powder granules, and capsule form. In any form it is tasteless. Many powdered protein supplements contain lecithin, from which you can make rather tasty shakes, or mix the protein-lecithin combination with fresh or frozen orange juice for a very good-flavored pick-me-up beverage.

CHEESE

No one argues that cheese is good for us, unless they are afraid of cholesterol, which we don't consider a valid concern. (See "Philosophy") It has a high NPU of about 70, and is high in

_____

8. Adele Davis, *Let's Cook It Right* (New York: Signet).

those amino acids which grains, cereals, nuts and seeds are usually low in: isoleucine and lysine. This makes it a good complementary protein to a plant protein.

Good cheese is made from certified raw milk produced from animals on farms that don't use pesticides or chemical fertilizers. These cheeses can often be found at health food stores. Other natural cheeses which are good and now available in the United States are Edam, Gouda, Provolone, and Swiss.

While natural cheese matures slowly through enzymatic action, processed cheeses are made quickly by heating and then aerating them to increase their volume. Very low quality cheese is usually used, which is ground and mixed in chemicals as emulsifiers. Beatrice Trum Hunter calls processed cheese a *plastic mass,* adding that *the end products have undergone such modifications that they scarcely deserve classification as good.*[9]

And you can't go by flavor either. In processed food, cheese flavor, as in TV snacks, doesn't mean cheese but a chemical flavor unrelated to nutrition. These flavor boosters are not at all related to cheese. They are a blend of imitation flavor, spices, salt, MSG, and sugar. It has been said of processed cheeses that *in the arrested state in which they reach the consumer they can easily survive him and sometimes do.*[10]

So much for processed cheese. What about cottage cheese? Here let us quote from *Prevention Magazine.*

> *Sodium hypochlorite may be used in the process of washing the curd. Diacetyl may. be added as a flavoring agent. Large amounts of salt may be added. Annatto (a dye derived from seeds) or cochineal (a dye derived from dried female insects) may be used as coloring agents. Hydrogen peroxide is frequently used as a preservative.*

------

9. Beatrice T. Hunter, *Consumer Beware* (New York: Simon and Schuster, 1971).

10. Vivienne Marquis and Patricia Haskell, *The Cheese Book* (New York: Simon and Schuster, 1965).

Calcium sulphate, which is related to plaster of paris, which has no nutritive value and is a material of questionable safety in foods, is permitted and usually used in cottage cheese. Mold retarders of sorbic acid are also permitted. Nothing but sorbic acid is required to be noted on the label.

The hydrogen peroxide is added to destroy bacteria as well as bleach the cheese. At the same time, it destroys vitamin A. Later, a catalase is added in order to remove the hydrogen peroxide. The wrapper on the cheese does not tell you what dyes have been used in order to color the product. Dairy interests are the only food processors legally exempted from the ruling that added color must be stated on the label. Blue or green coloring is sometimes added to white cheese to offset the natural yellow color.[11]

Are you convinced?

YOGURT

All yogurt is not good just because it bears the name yogurt. If it is made from old or pre-soured milk, or is embellished with synthetic flavors, sugar and artificial colorings, it won't be doing for you all you expect it to do.

Yogurt is one of the main foods in the diets of the people of the various European countries noted for their health and longevity. For example, 80 per cent of the diet of the people of Caucasus and the Balkan states is made up of cultured milk such as yogurt, and its sister, kefir. A 1970 census shows that there are 4,500 to 5,000 people in Caucasus who are over 100 years old. In Azerbaijan they make up 63 per 100,000 people, as compared with 3 centenarians per 100,000 population in the United States.

There seem to be many reasons why yogurt is so good for us. For one thing it contains friendly bacteria that contribute to better digestion and elimination. These bacteria are called the *intestinal flora,* and provide lactic acid needed for digestion in the stomach, as well as act as a protection against infection, since unwanted germs cannot live in an acid medium

---

11. Jane Kinderlehrer, "Cheese It," *Prevention* (April, 1973).

In fact, one of the greatest benefits of yogurt is its natural antibiotic effect. It contains penicillin, and has been found to destroy two types of human TB and one type of bovine TB. It has also been found effective against amoebic dysentary (used in enemas), typhus, S. paratyphus, Br. abortus, V. Comma, E. Subtilis, S. pullorum, S. dysentariae, P. vulgaris, M. pyrogenes, E. coli, K. pneumonia, streptococcus, staphylococcus, L. lactis, C. diptheriae, D. mitis, and S. fecalis.

It helps the intestinal flora already present to manufacture free vitamins such as the B Complex, especially niacin, riboflavin (B-2), biotin, folic acid, and vitamin K. The acid in the yogurt also aids in the assimilation of calcium, iron and protein.[12]

To be sure you are getting the best yogurts, buy them in health stores, since they are most likely to carry yogurts made from reliable sources of properly cultured milk. Avoid them if they are flavored with fruits or other flavoring unless they are natural. Synthetic additions are often *fed on* by the culture, which can pervert the product. There are good brands available that are made with honey for sweeteners.

Goat milk yogurt is good, and all the plain yogurts are a good sour cream substitute. Yogurt also makes a good sundae. Over a scoop of yogurt spoon homemade apple sauce (with honey, of course) or other fresh, honey-sweetened fruit, and top with wheat germ nuggets. (Hypoglycemics should be able to tolerate this, but test yourself with a little bit at a time.)

HONEY

We usually sweeten with honey. Honey is a completely natural, 100 per cent pure food. No bacteria can live in honey, and it contains no additives, preservatives, or adulterants. We do make sure, however, that we purchase raw honey rather than the kind (most often found in supermarkets) which has been heated. If honey has been heated, it will not turn crystalline, or *sugary*. Such granulation is normal, and will occur with age, and at temperatures ranging between 50 and 60 degrees Farenheit. This doesn't alter the content and flavor of

---

12. Linda Clark, M.A., "The Yogurt Controversy Revisited," *Let's Live* (May, 1973).

the honey, only its appearance, and this is easily remedied by placing the honey container in a vessel of warm water until the honey regains its liquid state.

The flavor of honey varies greatly according to the environmental conditions (primarily the relative humidity); the floral source; its ripeness when extracted (ripeness is determined by moisture content. Honey with 17 to 18 per cent moisture content will not ferment unless exposed to humid air long enough to absorb considerable moisture); methods used in extracting the honey from the combs; conditions of storage; as well as the pH and the mineral content of the soil. This means that you will obtain a greater variety of flavors in your breads and desserts made with honey. For instance, honey obtained from orange blossoms will give an orange flavor to the foods, while one from the eucalyptus trees would leave quite a different taste and aroma.

For the same reasons, the health-giving qualities of honey will vary accordingly. Honey contains enzymes, minerals, vitamins such as vitamin C, certain aromatic bodies which themselves contain essential oils, minute amounts of yeasts, and certain acids (said to be the reason buckwheat honey is dark in color and stringent in taste). Even the color varies according to the plant pigments, chlorophyll decomposition products, and colloidal particles. A high mineral content will produce a dark honey like heather or buckwheat honey, which has about four times as much iron as the light honeys like clover honey. Likewise, the Vitamin C content will vary according to the flowers used by the bees to make the honey.

When we say *processing* in reference to honey, we are referring to the way it is handled after it leaves the honeycombs, which can alter color, texture and clarity or lack of clarity. We do not refer to a heating process, or a procedure of additives. Regardless of appearance, which can be altered by temperature and humidity, honey will retain its basic health-giving qualities and purity.

Generally honey need not be refrigerated. However, since honey does contain sugar-tolerant yeasts, there are certain conditions which will cause fermentation. This is primarily determined by the moisture content of the honey. If it is above 18 per cent when extracted from the hive, or if the honey absorbs moisture beyond that percentage from the humid air, it can ferment. If this should happen, heat the honey at 145 degrees for one hour; then store in airtight containers.

An added desirable characteristic of honey is its ability to draw moisture out of the air. This makes it desirable in baking, since the product will remain naturally fresh and moist much longer.

Here are some terms used in relation to honey:

BLENDED means the honey derives from more than one type of flower. It may have been blended by the bees themselves, or by the honey handlers..

FILTERED means that the pollen grains have been removed by that process, which makes the honey clear and more aesthetic to look at. Unfiltered honey is cloudy because it still contains the pollen grains, which many people prefer because of the natural health-giving qualities of the pollen.

UNPROCESSED means that none of the food value has been removed, nor has anything been added.

Honey is uncooked and organic—it is made only by the bee, and is eaten raw by us. Raw honey is honey which is as close to its original state as possible. It is honey that the bees themselves eat. And since no bacteria can live in honey, and it contains no additives or preservatives, it is pure.

One of the reasons honey is a preferred sweetener is that its sugars are in invert form, which means that they are readily assimilated since they have already been partially digested by the bees themselves in their honey-stomachs. Honey is also not habit forming, which refined sugar can be, due to the explosive effect the refined sugar has on the digestive system. Sugar is a powerful stimulant that burns at intense heat, and then dies out quickly, which produces a *let-down* in the body, making the body demand more sugar to raise the blood sugar level to normal. But since more sugar will produce the same effect again—rapid and intense raising of the blood sugar, a vicious merry-go-round is started in the body, producing undue strain. This can make poorly-nourished persons highly susceptible to sugar addiction. Such people have been called *sugar-holics.*

Honey has also been used for medicinal purposes throughout man's history. It has been used for treatment of cuts and burns, as a remedy for gastric and intestinal disorders, in treating respiratory disorders such as hay fever and asthma, as a salve for skin diseases such as poison ivy and smallpox, for inflammation of the eyes and eyelids, as a tranquilizer, to help miagrain headaches, and it has been used on surgical dressings.

One can see how it might be an effective anitbiotic since no bacteria can live in honey. In a test situation, bacteria introduced into honey died in a short time. The honey absorbed the moisture from the bacteria and dehydrated them to their deaths.

As far as we know, no mention has ever been made of anyone being allergic or sensitive to honey, or having suffered any serious consequences as a result of using honey internally or externally.

COOKING WITH HONEY

MEASURING HONEY: Since honey is sticky, we recommend first measuring the oil to be used in the recipe, or run the measuring device under water first. The oil works best, and the honey will slip right out. If you are concerned with exact measurements of honey, you will have to level the top of *the measuring cup with a spatula, since honey tends to round-out* in a spoon or cup before it drips over. However, since different honeys seem to vary in taste, if not in sweetness, we don't concern ourselves with exact measurements.

Since honey is a liquid rather than a solid like sugar, we recommend reducing the amount of liquid used, or increasing the amount of dry ingredients used. Often a dash of wheat germ will take care of this. Generally, reduce the liquid by one-quarter cup for each cup of honey used.

We find that substituting honey for sugar cup for cup, although they are supposed to have the same sweetness level, often makes the food too sweet. This is an individual preference, and you will want to experiment. We generally use one-half to three-fourths the amount of honey as sugar called-for.

For example, in a recipe calling for one cup sugar, we would use three-fourths cup, or even only one-half cup honey, depending on the food being prepared. In custards, which are mildly flavored, and which readily reflect the strong flavor of honey and the extra sweetness, we use half as much honey as sugar called for in the recipe. In foods with strong flavors of their own, such as cakes and cookies, we will often substitute honey cup for cup.

It pays to remember that foods made with honey brown faster than those made with sugar, since the fruit sugar in honey carmelizes at high temperatures. It is a good idea to reduce the calle-for temperature by at least 25 degreesn when substituting honey for sugar.

Since honey draws moisture from the air, cakes and cookies made with honey will be tender and moist. In fact, don't expect to make crisp cookies with honey. The honey will continue to absorb moisture and flavors from other foods, so keep the food stored separately or wrapped in foil or plastic.

Baked goods made with honey will be more flavorful. You may want to make them a day ahead of when you plan to serve them, since they will taste better the second day.

Section IV
Helps & Hints

Section IV
HELPS & HINTS

WHAT TO THROW OUT

Now that you have a kitchenful of good things, you can throw these out:

1. *refined white and brown sugar.*
2. *bleached and unbleached white flour, and their companion products.*
3. *shortenings that are solid at room temperature.*
4. *white rice, and pastas like spaghetti, macaroni and noodles made with white flour.*
5. *refined table salt.*
6. *any product containing preservatives, including the so-called freshness preservers BHA and BHT.*
7. *any food containing sugar, especially fruits canned in heavy syrup.*
8. *all packaged dry cereals except Grape Nuts and Roman Meal hot cereal. (Some store granolas may be alright, but your own homemade would be better.)*
9. *hydrogenated peanut butters.*
10. *all synthetic sweeteners and any products made with them.*
11. *any candies and commercial breads that use emulsifiers and preservatives. There are some commercial breads that use honey rather than sugar and use no preservatives. These breads won't feel gluey and stick to your mouth when eaten.*
12. *maraschino cherries, probably the worst food on the market. They are almost all sugar and artificial chemicals.*
13. *chocolate: Chocolate is naturally bitter. To produce the sweet chocolate we are used to, 40 per cent white refined sugar is added. It is high in fat and calories. 100 grams (3½*

oz.) contain 528 calories, as compared to 180 calories for the same amount of carob. Chocolate also contains a stimulant chemically related to caffeine, called theobromine, plus caffeine itself. These, especially in children, can become addictive. Since chocolate contains oxalic acid, which combines with the calcium, it interferes with absorption of calcium, a problem for all ages. Thus, adding chocolate to milk actually decreases its nutritive value. It is often an important factor in cavity formation, as well as allergies. Finally, the processing is so thorough that while chocolate contains concentrated and excessive calories, there is no nutritive value at all.

MESSAGE TO HYPOGLYCEMICS

Initially this book was intended for hypoglycemics who were discouraged by the bleak prospects of living on the Seal-Harris diet, which most patients don't fully understand. In fact, about all it means to them is that there is nothing for them to eat.

For our readers who don't suffer from low blood sugar and who are wondering what the long word means, let us explain. Basically hypoglycemia is chronic low blood sugar, apparently due to pancreatic irregularity. It is said to be the opposite of diabetes, since there is too much insulin in the blood stream. To avoid going into shock from the insulin, the body throws substances from the adrenal cortex into the blood stream. Finally, if this continues repetitious stress on the adrenal gland becomes too much for it and it ceases to function properly.

One can be born hypoglycemic, or can develop it later. It can also be brought on by undue stress and when this is the cause it will usually go away when the stress is over. But the chronic low blood sugar is not so easily handled, and requires adherence to proper diet, and occasionally intravenous injections of natural adrenal cortex extract from goats, which takes over the function of the adrenal gland for a short period of time, allowing it complete rest.

It seems that poor eating habits and stress can bring on the symptoms, while at times it appears that the malnutrition came afterward as a result of the body being unable to cope. This area seems to be open for speculation. Maybe, like Dr. Fredricks' theory of diabetes, it is triggered by a liver malfunction due to overconsumption of highly processed carbohydrates and sugar.

An article in Diabetes[1] states that the performance of the liver determines the outcome of the glucose tolerance test, suggesting that the liver is more important than the pancreas in controlling blood sugar. (Note: This makes the vitamin B-complex from a natural source critical for a diabetic or a hypoglycemic. Of the three sources, brewer's yeast, wheat germ, and desiccated liver, the liver is the most common. Prior to the advent of insulin, doses of liver were used to help control blood sugar levels.)

Most cases of hypoglycemia indicate a latent or pre-diabetic stage and it is believed that all diabetics were once hypoglycemic. It is interesting that if your mother was hypoglycemic, chances are you will be. One explanation is that she used your adrenal gland during pregnancy, explaining why hypoglycemic women feel their best when they are pregnant. Such a strain on the adrenal gland of the developing baby apparently creates the adrenal cortical insufficiency characteristic of low blood sugar.

It is complicated to understand, and all the information is not in on it. But if you already have it, proper diet will control it, and if you don't have it, chances are that with proper diet you won't develop it.

There are as many symptoms connected with low blood sugar as there are people who suffer from it. Some very general ones include continued fatigue and illness, unexplainable infections and allergies, headaches, chronic nervousness, shaking, inability to concentrate, emotional disorders, including amnesia and lying, and lack of shame, pessimism, and continual hunger pangs. There are many more, and all of these symptoms don't need to be present to indicate low blood sugar.

We wonder if a great many of the problems of today's children can be traced to some degree of hypoglycemia. We do know that 9 out of 10 of the overweight children in the United States today are hypoglycemic. It has been suggested that with our modern processed quick foods which lack nutritional value, and our tremendous consumption of processed carbohydrates and refined sugar (over 100 pounds of sugar per year per person), most Americans probalbly have the illness to

---

1. Diabetes XXII (June 1973), 442-58.

some extent. The struggle to digest such large quantities of carbohydrates with no outside help becomes too much for the body and it ceases to be capable of handling the dead, chemically un-nutritive carbohydrates that are shoved into it in a continual barrage.

We are hypoglycemic and can eat all the food we include in this book. We eat often, in small amounts, and use whole, natural foods. When we get a headache after eating, we know we've either eaten the wrong food or too much of a particular food. Our tolerance to certain natural carbohydrates varies, and a headache is our warning. Generally, a good, concentrated protein will take care of the problem. (Going too long without food can cause the same headache.)

In day-to-day living we can't or won't take time to count and add up units of protein, carbohydrates and such. Our advice to the hypoglycemic is to eat whole BALANCED natural foods, with a preponderance of protein, often, in small amounts, and with attention to your body's reaction. Nervousness, or headache, or an uncomfortable, itchy tingling in the legs, or nausea, could all be signs that you have eaten something wrong, or too much of something right. Watch your own body carefully—learn its language; then experiment with your kind and quantity of food to find out what you can tolerate. Don't forget that your tolerance level can change from day to day.

One problem with the disorder is that not enough patients take it seriously. One doctor has said that diabetics are the most difficult patients because they don't take their illness seriously, and as a result a disproportionate number of them die needlessly from it. Well, many hypoglycemics find it even harder to take themselves seriously, especially when most medical doctors pooh-pooh the problem calling it a fad, or worse, oft-times telling the patient not to worry about it because it is nothing serious.

An airline pilot we know was diagnosed as hypoglycemic, but the doctor told him not to worry about it because it wasn't serious, and he offered no treatment or routine for control. One day the pilot blacked-out while he was working on the airplane. Some knowledgeable person gave him first-aid and saved his life. But he lost his job, and a substantial income that would have amounted to a great deal of money by retirement time. (He was a young man.)

The only adequate test for determining low blood sugar is the five or six-hour glucose tolerance test. Any simple one-step blood test is not sufficient for diagnosis; And not all doctors agree on how to read the results.

Hypoglycemia has been accused as the villain in many crimes of violence and in many emotional disturbances.

SUGGESTED READINGS

CONFESSIONS OF A SNEAKY ORGANIC COOK, by Jane Kinderlehrer, Rodale Press, Signet Book, New American Library Inc., 1301 Avenue of the Americas, New York, 10019.

A most entertaining introduction into the why's of good food, and the results of their absence from the diet. She tells how to sneak the good things into the food you serve. She explains why certain foods are good for you, as well as describes the symptoms of specific vitamin and mineral deficiencies. Her style is so conversational you feel that she is sitting across the table talking to you over a glass of juice. This is a good beginner book for learning why we should eat better.

NATURAL FOODS COOKBOOK, by Beatrice Trum Hunter.

You will find a number of true health-food recipes, including an especially good chapter on cooking organ meats. There is an introduction to each chapter giving some basic information about the foods included in that chapter, and any general or special techniques used in their preparation. One section lists the sources, Including addresses for hard-to-get health-food items from around the country. And the recipes she offers are good.

DIET FOR A SMALL PLANET, by Frances Moore Lappe, Friends of the Earth/Ballantine Book, 101 Fifth Avenue, New York, 10003.

Here author Lappe presents an argument that the grams of protein in a food are not adequate indicators of the protein value of that food, since only protein in certain combinations can be used by the body. She presents charts showing the actual protein utilization of the different foods, suggesting the use of complementary plant proteins to replace meat protein, thereby obtaining protein quality equal to, and often exceeding, that of meat, but from sources cheaper, and lower on the food chain. She also includes charts showing the best buys per unit of usable protein, and the best choices of food calorie-wise per unit of usable protein. If you already understand her thesis, the book is worth buying for the charts. *WHEAT AND SUGAR FREE*, by Frieda H. Nusz, Pine Hill Press, Freeman, South Dakota, 57029.

Mrs. Nusz provides recipes that don't need sugar or wheat, though wheat can be used in any of them. All preparation is in the blender, which she feels is the convenient way to prepare foods today. She also tells what to do and what not to do with the blender. These blender hints are helpful, and the recipes we've tried have all been good.

THE LOW BLOOD SUGAR COOKBOOK, by Margo Blevin and Geri Ginder, Doubleday and Company, Inc., Garden City, New York.

This book is a collection of hundreds of recipes following the Seale-Harris diet for hypoglycemia. They restrict many of the foods we include, and include many which we restrict, such as Sanka, saccharin, and diet sodas. But for a good variety of dishes for all occasions this is a helpful book. (Hard cover only)

BODY, MIND AND SUGAR by E. M. Abrahamson, M.D., and A. W. Pezet, Pyramid Publications, 444 Madison Avenue, New York, NY 10022.

NATURAL HEALTH, SUGAR AND THE CRIMINAL MIND, J. I. Rodale, Pyramid Publications (same as above.)

LOW BLOOD SUGAR AND YOU, Carleton Fredericks, PhD., and Herman Goodman, M.D., Constellation International, 51 Madison Avenue, New York, NY 10022.

GET WELL NATURALLY, Linda Clark, Arc Books Inc., 219 Park Avenue South, New York, NY 10003.

ECOLOGY NOW

While we are against government enforcement of environment protection, since it is not within the legitimate scope of government, we are for individual responsibility in using the environment in ways that benefit both Mother Nature and Man.

Actually, our thesis here benefits Man more than Mother Nature, while allowing Mother Nature her full course. It is simple. Don't throw away any food. Not only will your health and the health of your yard improve, but you won't nee a garbage disposal.

All liquids left from cooking, sprouting or soaking go into a stock jar. Keep a plastic sack in the refrigerator for the solid items, such as cores, bones, left-overs, scraps, and when each meal preparation is finished, throw these *left-overs* into the bag. When the bag is full, put the contents into a pan, cover with water and simmer over low heat, covered, for a few hours. Strain, and pour into glass jars, like old peanut butter jars, instant drink jars, whatever—cover and refrigerate. Bones can be cooked the same way for soup or for the stock jar. When stock begins to pile up, freeze some, or use it in place of water when making new stock. Just be sure to use your own judgment. An already strong stock doesn't need to become more concentrated.

Stock is used any place you would have used water before, except for steaming, of course. It can be added to vegetable juices for extra nutrients, and can be used to make instant vegetable soup. (See recipe)

All the egg shells (they contain calcium) and remaining stock-pot solids and burned toast, or whatever of that nature, can go into a compost heap in an obscure corner of your yard. This is a planned *garbage dump* where food leftovers, raked leaves, grass cuttings, and anything else organic you can think of (except human and raw animal feces) is thrown. Some steer manure is good, too. Keep the pile moist, and turn it occasionally, if it's feasible. Be sure to bury any food that the flies may want to lay eggs in. At the end of the year that *garbage heap* will be a rich pile of humus that looks, feels and smells like earth from the deepest part of a virgin forest. And none of us needs to be told what to do with rich soil.[2]

Seeds from fresh fruits and vegetables can be simmered in stock. (Taste them first. Some are bitter.) or added to the food the vegetable is used in. For example add the pepper seeds to the salad, or to the filling for the stuffed pepper. Dried seeds can be planted, or fed to the birds in winter, or added to the compost heap.

Seeds having the flavor of almonds, such as apricot, peach and apple seeds are said to contain vitamin B-17, a nitrilocide called laetrile in its synthesized form, and considered in many countries and by many cancer patients here in the United

---

2. There are more scientific descriptions of how to make a compost heap, but this will get you started, and you can develop finer techniques later.

States to be a cancer control. The U.S. government is against the use of laetrile, on the grounds that since it isn't toxic it can't be useful in cancer. They admit that it is non-toxic and harmless. But they refuse to do any in-depth research on it, and unfortunately, it has entered the field of politics. We suppose this is why you often hear warnings that these seeds are poisonous. No hard evidence has been offered toward this claim that we are aware of, and many people eat them regularly without apparent effects of poisoning.

In fact, according to Dr. Ernest Krebs, Jr., discoverer of B-17, and synthesizer of laetrile, the fruit of the apple, for example used to contain traces of nitrilocides (B-17, laetrile) so that one could get all he wanted by eating just the fruit. Today there are no traces left in the fruit itself, due, we suspect, to the agricultural methods that have devitalized so many of our foods.

So we eat the seeds, and ignore the warning that the natural laetrile in the seeds can be toxic when the government admits that the synthetic laetrile is non-toxic.[3]

STEAMING VEGETABLES

We recommend that all vegetables be steamed rather than boiled or simmered or baked, so that water and air touch them as little as possible. Here are the basic instructions on preparing fresh vegetables by steaming.

Add a few inches of water to the pan, place vegetable steamer in the pan and add vegetables to the steamer. Turn heat to medium and cover. When water simmers, turn heat back to low or warm (depending on your cooking utensils and individuality of your stove) so that cooking continues but the water does not boil. Let them steam cook until they are warmed through but still crisp. To serve, sprinkle with lemon, or salt with sea salt or kelp, or use both, and add pepper. We recommend adding pepper after food is cooked since heat can quickly turn the pepper into an inorganic substance that is hard to digest. Save the stock from the steaming and put in your stock jar.

---

3. The apparent active ingredient of the nitrilocides is arsenic. But it is bound up into the laetrile in such a way that the body does not allow it to be released except in the location of a cancer tumor.

If you don't have a steamer, and can't afford to buy one of the kind available in department stores and specialty shops and variety stores, then use just enough water to cover the bottom of the pan, turn heat to medium and add vegetables. Cover. When water simmers, turn heat back, or off, and cook as above. Check occasionally to see if more water is needed.

It is harder to cook without the steamer, and you will have to experiment, keeping in mind the four *robbers* of food nutrients: paring knife, air, water, and heat.

Some brands of stainless cookware have a steamer combination consisting of what looks like a double boiler, but with the bottom of the top pan full of holes like a colander.[4] These are best of all.

SPROUTS

Sprouts of seeds will give the highest food value possible for seeds to offer. As the seed, the essence of life, begins to sprout, vitamins, minerals, and enzymes are formed. Their nutritional value skyrockets, with the most spectacular rise in vitamin C. A sprouting soybean sees an increase of 553 per cent. Other vitamins jump too, and pyridoxine and pantothenic acid, usually short-changed in synthetic formulations, triple in the sprouts. Some seeds develop complete protein patterns capable of sustaining life. And the carbohydrate content is very low.

And they can be conveniently grown on your kitchen counter or under the sink, supplying fresh greens year-round, without reliance on a store or a yard.

Jane Kinderlerhrer begins her discussion on sprouts in her book with this question:

What is it that rivals meat for protein, has more vitamin C than tomatoes, supplies practically all the nutrients your body needs, has no waste at all in preparation, requires little or no fuel to prepare, can be

---

4. For information write: Saladmaster of Utah
PO Box 20401
Granger, Utah 84120

*used on land or sea, or in snow-bound villages, and can
be produced almost like magic as needed?*[5]

Sprouting is not difficult. Remember what the conditions
are in a garden for a seed to grow: warmth but no heat,
moisture, but not flooding, and protection from sun and the dry
air. Then proceed to sprout your seeds, grains and beans
keeping these conditions in mind.

SPROUTING BEANS: Sprouting beans not only
increases their food value, but also prevents that after-eating
gas problem we associate with cooked beans. Unless, of
course, in the process of cooking you overheat the beans, and
the high temperature kills the sprouts.

Wash the beans and soak as usual, covering beans with
water, and let stand for 8 hours, or overnight. They will soak up
the water, so check them periodically to make sure they are still
covered with the water. Drain beans, put liquid in stock jar, and
place beans in stainless or plastic colander dish. Cover with
dish towel (non-terry if possible, since the sprouts will want to
grow to the terry and they will be hard to remove), and let stand.
Occasionally check them to see that they are moist. The towel
is to keep the air off them to prevent the air from drying them
out, and the holes in the colander allow for drainage. In a day
and a half to two days the sprouts will be as long as the bean
and they are ready to be cooked in the juice you saved in the
stock jar.

SPROUTING SEEDS: There are numerous sprouting
sets on the market today, available in many different kinds of
stores. These are convenient to use. If you can't afford to buy
one, or can't find one, or prefer to do it on your own, a glass jar
will do just fine (except for mung bean sprouts). Fill jar one
third full of seeds, cover with water and soak overnight. Cover
mouth of the jar with some cheesecloth, held on by a rubber
band. Drain, and save stock in stock jar. Tip sprout jar uhside
down at a slant, and let drain. Keep in dark place. Check
occasionally to make sure seeds are moist, and gently shake jar
to keep sprouts from growing into a tangled mass. If more

---

5. Jane Kinderlehrer, *Confessions of a Sneaky Organic
   Cook,* p. 20.

water is needed, hold jar with cloth still on top under faucet and fill with warm water, then drain immediately. Place jar back at upside down slant and they will drain and continue to grow. When the sprout of wheat is as long as the seed, and when the sprout of the seed becomes bright green, they are ready. Remove the cheesecloth, cover with lid, and store in refrigerator. Some, like the wheat sprout, will continue to grow.

MUNG BEAN SPROUTS: These require darkness, moisture added three times a day, (with good drainage) and a weight on top, so they think they are pushing up against the earth. Without this weight, and with light, the sprout gets too bitter before it gets large enough to eat. The mung bean is a mild sprout, and one of the most popular. It is available in the grocery stores in the produce section. These have the *shell* washed off. Whether you wash the *shell* off is up to you; some say it should be washed and some insist it shouldn't.

We recommend sprouting these in the colander as well, but that you also place a dish on top whose weight will spread out over the entire top of the beans. Then put them under the sink or in a closet where no sunlight can get to them, and be sure to water them three times a day. When the sprouts are about two inches long, they are ready to eat.

Remember to use only certified, organically grown seeds. Most commercial seeds have been treated with chemicals, and besides not wanting to ingest these chemicals, we think chemical treatment sometimes affects their sprouting capability.

BEVERAGES

Juices and Spas
Milk and buttermilk (raw)
Pero
Protein Shakes
Hot Carob
Herb Teas
Root Beer
"Honegar"

We avoid caffeine, high-acid beverages, and sugared drinks. Here's what we drink.

JUICES: Health food stores carry a variety of fruit juices that are unsweetened and as raw as possible. Grape juice and apple juice are especially good tasting, though hypoglycemics will have to test their tolerance to the grape juice. Unsweetened grapefruit and pineapple juices can also be found in most grocery stores, and many snack bars and coffee shops carry unsweetened citrus juices for you to drink when others order soft drinks and coffee.

ORANGE SPA: To give an extra kick to pineapple or orange juice, add powdered protein and serve a Spa.

ORANGE SPA

In blender put one large can frozen orange juice and three cans water. Blend. Add 1/3 cup protein powder. Blend again and serve. This is a good snack drink with peanut butter sandwiches and egg sandwiches. Usually children like this drink more than they do the plain juice.

MILK AND BUTTERMILK: We do not recommend buttermilk unless it is fresh from the country. Commercial buttermilk will last many weeks in the refrigerator, while fresh buttermilk without any additives lasts only a few days, after which it must be used in cooking. We prefer not to drink whatever preservatives are used to prevent spoilage in the commercial brands.

We prefer raw milk since, as we mentioned before, pasteurizing milk kills the lecithin which we need. Today's cows are kept disease-free and are milked under sanitary conditions, so that certified raw milk is healthy and safe. The children can't taste the difference, and won't know the difference unless someone tells them. Goat's milk is also good, though a little stronger in flavor, depending on the grasses it has been eating, and we've been told that horse milk is very sweet. Raw goat's milk is naturally homogenized, and has been used very successfully in treatment of arthritis.

PERO: Pero is a coffee substitute that tastes the closest to coffee that we have found. It is a roasted rye and barley beverage that has no caffeine. It is a German product, but can be found in most supermarkets in the coffee sections, and usually can be found in specialty shops and delicatessens. Drink it as you would coffee, black, or with honey, or with honey and milk.

PROTEIN SHAKE: Experiment with this, adapting it to different moods and tastes. Here is a basic recipe.

Protein Shake: Fill blender 2/3 full with water. Add and blend:

1-1/2 cups protein powder
1/4 cup wheat germ
1/4 cup carob powder
1/4 cup food yeast
1/4 - 1/3 cup honey

Optional: raw egg, cinnamon, nutmeg, vanilla. Change these proportions according to your taste. It isn't always the world's best shake, but often it is a good way to stifle hunger pangs quickly and nutritiously. For that morning you don't have time for breakfast it will be a nutritious substitute. Keep some already blended in a jar in the refrigerator.

As we stated in our introduction, we are only interested in getting you started using these foods. There are many proven and tried shakes to be found in the different cookbooks available that you might want to try, and your own imagination will concoct some good ones. We offer a starter.

HOT CAROB: Carob tastes similar to chocolate when it is roasted. Unless otherwise stated, the carob you buy will be roasted. It isn't as strong a flavor as chocolate, but it is better for you. We have excluded chocolate from our diets.

Directions: in each cup put one heaping teaspoon carob, fill with hot water (or fill half and half with hot water and raw milk). Add a heaping teaspoon of raw honey, a dash of vanilla, and stir well. A touch of cinnamon will add a Mexican flavor. Since this is not an instant powder, the carob will tend to settle in the bottom of the cup, and will need to be stirred from time to time while you are drinking it.

ROOTBEER

1/3 bottle root beer extract
1-1/2 cups raw honey
1-1/2 t. yeast granules
1 cup lukewarm water

Place all ingredients in the blender. Mix on lowest speed until yeast is dissolved. Pour into gallon jug and add cool water to fill jug to within one inch of the top. Place lid on lightly and let set at room temperature for at least 24 hours. It is best when left for three or four days. Tighten lid and refrigerate at least eight hours before serving.

WINE

"What about wine?" we're asked. "Does it fit into the natural food category?"

With the chemicals and sugar used in making wine today one can't classify wine as a natural food, and its value as a health beverage is controversial. There are physicians who believe that wine has definite physiological values, including goodly amounts of the B-vitamin complex and vitamin P, which strenghtens the capillaries, as well as traces of almost all of the thirteen major mineral elements, including potassium, magnesium and calcium, being especially high in iron while having very little sodium. It has been used to treat fatigue and as a protective factor against coronary disease. As a natural tranquilizer and a stimulant to appetite it is probably to be preferred over chemical drugs.

However, while pointing out certain health factors wine can have we do not intend to promote its consumption as a beverage. It does contain alcohol, which the body must detoxify. This is done primarily by the liver, an organ already much overworked in its attempts to detoxify the body of chemical pollutants from the smoggy air we breathe and the chemically fertilized, processed, colored and preserved foods most Americans eat every day. It is an added strain for the diabetic or hypoglycemic since a dysfunctioning liver is an important contributing factor in blood sugar abnormalities.

And let's not forget that sugar is often used in making wines (an additional strain on the liver), especially the cheaper brands. Chemicals may be used to hurry the fermentation process and to preserve the final product. It is for these same reasons we do not drink soft drinks of any kind.

HONEGAR: As a mealtime drink which is full of nutrients and aids digestion, we suggest honegar. This is a mixture of half raw honey and half good-quality cider vinegar. Add 1 tablespoon of mixture to an 8-ounce glass and fill with water. Stir and drink. This is also a mild tranquilizer because of the honey.

Most of us have some trouble with digestion, which often we are not aware of. The result is that the body is not using the food we put into it, or is using only a part of it. That is why we do not recommend drinking with a meal, unless it is honegar. Other beverages slow down the stomach's ability to digest thoroughly. Milk itself is not easily digested (in fact, many people are allergic to it because they lack the lactase enzyme needed for digestion), and water will dilute the stomach digestive acid.

In the *olden days* people did suffer from over-acidity, but our processed foods which are very alkaline, our problem is usually one of over-alkalinity. Honegar will help. If a stomach ache appears as a result, you can be quite sure you really need it. Just take small amounts at first.

Honegar is a source of the vitamins, minerals and enzymes found in raw honey and cider vinegar, so it is nutritious as well. We can even use it straight, mixed wih cayenne and ginger for sore throats. It is also a good liquid to help you swallow your supplements.

Honegar is a fast, sparkling substitute for those dashes of sugar we used to add to spaghetti and mayonnaise and the like. Dried mint soaked in honegar several hours makes a quick, good mint sauce for lamb.

Just keep a bottle of the made-up honegar on hand. In cooking, use full-strength. For dinking, add water to taste, usually 1 tablespoon to eight ounces of water.

PRESERVES

We make our sauces and syrups for pancake and waffle toppings. We don't use pectin for jams and jellies since the commercial brands we have checked have sugar as a main ingredient, and since we have not had the time to make our own pectin from apples, though this is possible. Also, while some people tell us that they can get their fruits to thicken with the commercial pectin, our experience has been that the use of raw honey inhibits the thickening process. So we use the juice of the fruits, add honey to taste, heat to simmer, and bottle like jam. This is our syrup. The pulp left after the juice is made we combine with honey, using about half what the recipe calls for in sugar, and heat to simmering. Then we bottle it in the usual way.

It may be possible to simmer the fruit juice and honey for making syrup for many hours, with a thickening occuring eventually. This works with cranberry sauce. If you prefer a thicker syrup, try this, but make sure the fire is low and the syrup is only simmering.

When cold-packing fruit, we don't make a sugar syrup. Instead, we pack the jars as usual, dribble a heaping tablespoon of raw honey over the top of the fruit, and then pour boiling water into the jar until the jar is full. The water dissolves the honey as it goes into the jar, and with honey there is no need to add cit ic acid to prevent discoloration. Then we cold-pack as usual.

Here are included two raw recipes—one for mincemeat and one for delicious, tangy tomato relish that tastes like hot dog relish and is delicious on top of tamales, or mixed into chili beans or black beans.

CHILI RELISH

8 quarts (1 peck) ripe tomatoes, skinned
6 green peppers
2 or 3 chili peppers
12 large onions
12 sweet red peppers

Put the above ingredients through a food chopper. Add 1 cup sea salt. Stir until salt is dissolved. Put mixture into sack and drain overnight. Then add:

2 T. mustard seed
4 cups cider vinegar
5 cups raw honey

Mix well. Let stand one hour; then bottle. Sealing isn't necessary.

RAW MINCEMEAT

2 lbs. fresh apples, chopped
rind of one orange, grated (if organically grown, otherwise no orange rind)
1 orange, finely diced
2 cups fresh or frozen pineapple juice (or canned, unsweetened)
1 lb seeds raisins
1 lb. currants
1 lb. golden raisins or an equal amount of chopp‑ed dates
1/2 lb. raw almonds or pecans
1/4 cup apple juice
2 t. cinnamon
1/2 t. cardamon
2 t. vanilla
1 t. nutmeg
1/2 t. allspice

Be sure the fruits are not treated chemically.
Peel, dice and measure apples into pineapple juice. Add diced orange and rind. Mix well. Stir in other fruits, and sliced nuts. In small saucepan mix together the apple juice and spices. Simmer for one minute. Mix into the fruits and add vanilla. When well mixed, place in covered freezer containers and let stand, refrigerated, for two or three days to develop the flavor. Freeze until needed. Remove from freezer 24 hours before serving. Serve with favorite hot sauce or top with whipped cream.

Section V
Recipes and
Planned Meals

RECIPES & PLANNED MEALS

BREAKFASTS

Breakfast is the most important meal of the day, and the least fun to fix. Following are menus and recipes for more than two full weeks. When the two weeks have been used, start over.

We have been vague about the fruits to be used, because the availability of fruits varies with the season, and because we didn't want the cook to have to buy seven different fruits for seven different days. In summer you might choose cherries, raspberries, pineapple, plums, grapes, melons, peaches and apricots, and in winter you could choose oranges, grapefruit, or unsweetened orange, pineapple, or grapefruit juice. When fresh fruits are hard to find in winter, use dried fruits, available in health specialty shops. The dried fruits found in most supermarkets are chemically dried and should be avoided. Eventually you may want to dry your own.

Choose your breakfast beverage from our section on beverages. Sometimes we offer suggestions, but the choice is up to you. As we said in the beginning, we are not trying to impress the reader with a tremendous variety of foods and drinks. We could name different breakfast fruit and different beverages for every day of the week. But in day-to-day living we don't buy seven different fruits for seven different days, and we usually prefer the same breakfast drink every day. And we do have leftovers.

We want to help the cook who has to prepare three meals a day. This means making things as simple and realistic as possible. Thus, reading our menus isn't terribly exciting. But they will be easy to follow and use day after day.

DAY ONE

MENU: *Corn Cakes*

Sliced Fresh Peaches
with raw honey and lecithin granules

Peppermint Tea or Coffee Substitute

CORN CAKES

Blend in order given: (use high speed)

3 fertile eggs
1 t. sea salt
1 cup raw milk (or reconstituted powdered milk,
or goat milk or soy milk)
1 cup corn meal
1/2 cup oil (preferably corn oil)
1 T. low sodium baking powder

The batter will be very thin. Pour batter into oiled skillet to make pancakes of desired size. Batter should be stirred briefly before each addition. Turn when top is bubbly. Serve with lots of butter and raw honey. A special treat is molasses added to the honey for a caramel taste. Use 1 - 2 T molasses per 1 cup raw honey, or less molasses for just a brown sugar taste.

DAY TWO

MENU: *Baked Eggs*

Whole Grain Toast

Unsweetened Pineapple Juice

Coffee Substitute

BAKED EGGS

Use individual casseroles, or stainless steel or glass cake or pie pan. Cover the bottom with oil. For each serving add:

2 fertile eggs
1/2 tomato, diced
1/4 green pepper, diced

Season with:

sea salt
dash chili powder or cayenne
rosemary
sweet basil

Top with 1/4 cup tomato sauce. Bake at 200 just until eggs are done. Top with generous sprinkle of wheat germ nuggets and Parmesan cheese. (These could also be steamed in a pan on top the stove, with the pan placed over simmering water, and covered.)

DAY THREE

MENU: *Panamanian French Toast*

Sliced fresh peaches

Peppermint Herb Tea or Coffee Substitute

PANAMANIAN FRENCH TOAST

Beat 3 fertile eggs
Add 1/2 cup raw milk, or reconstituted powdered milk
Stir in 2 t. cinnamon

Soak whole grain bread in the batter, making sure the moisture works all the way through. Toast slowly in corn oil in heavy skillet. Serve with raw honey, honey-jam, or homemade toppings. Serves 2.

DAY FOUR

MENU: *Millet*

Sliced Melon

Chilled unsweetened apple juice

MILLET

1 cup ground millet
3 cups cold water

Grind millet in electric grinder or buy millet pre-ground. Place millet and water in saucepan, stir well, and add 1 t. sea salt. Heat over low heat, stirring often to prevent lumpiness.

Once millet begins to thicken, it does so quickly. It will be the consistency of cream of wheat when it is done. Then add:

> 1 T. butter
> 11/2 T. raw honey
> 1/4 t. cinnamon

Serve in cereal bowl with some or all of these:

> sunflower seeds
> sesame seeds
> chopped nuts
> dried fruit
> raisins or currents
> fresh fruit

Sprinkle the top with wheat germ nuggets. Serves three.

DAY FIVE

MENU: *Steamed wheat or steamed Triticale[1]*

   Cinnamon-Honey Butter

   Sliced fruit in Season

   Peppermint Herb Tea or Coffee Substitute

STEAMED GRAINS

> 1 cup grain berries
> water to cover
> 1/4 t. sea salt

Place grain (wheat, triticali, or other choice) in upper pan of double boiler. Cover with water. In the bottom pan place as much water as it will hold, since it will simmer at least eight hours. If the pan isn't very large you may have to occasionally add boiling water to the bottom to prevent the pan from going dry and burning.

Place the double boiler, covered, on medium heat until water simmers. Turn the heat as low as possible, and preferably put a wire butterfly rack under the pan over the burner. (Make

---

1. These should be cooked overnight.

one by bending a wire coat hanger into a butterfly-shape.) This allows for the least heat possible going to the pan.

Steam overnight, or eight hours. Before serving, add 1 T. food yeast. VERY LITTLE heat is required. If you have a gas stove with a pilot light you can leave it on the pilot light over night. Some do nothing more than pour boiling water into a thermos, add the grain and cover, letting stand overnight. The grain will steam by this method, but it isn't quite so tender.

CINNAMON—HONEY BUTTER

Warm together in a measuring cup placed in a pan of simmering water:

1 cup raw honey
2 T. butter
1/2 t. cinnamon

NOTE: To get the most out of grains like wheat, you should complement them with other protein to raise the usability of the isoleucine and lysine amino acids. The food yeast will do this. If the taste is too different, milk can be served with it, and if you can't have milk, serve the grain with a soft-boiled egg.

DAY SIX

MENU: *Sam's Pancakes*

Fresh Fruit in Season

Raspberry Leaf Herb Tea or Coffee Substitute

SAM'S PANCAKES

Mix together:

3 fertile eggs
1/2 cup sunflower seeds, ground[2]
1/2 cup pumpkin seeds, ground[3]
1/4 cup corn meal
1/4 cup whole wheat flour
1/3 cup wheat germ

2, 3. Grind in a small electric coffee grinder.

2 T. wheat germ oil or soy or safflower oil
1/2 cup sour milk[4]
1 t. sea salt
1 T. cinnamon
1/4 t. nutmeg

Fry in heavy, oiled skillet. You will be surprised how filling they are.

DAY SEVEN

MENU: *Alfalfa Butter Eggs*

Sprouted Wheat Toast

Honey-Jam

Peppermint Herb Tea or Pero

ALFALFA OUTTER EGGS

In butter, fry eggs as you normally do, topping with alfalfa sprouts. Remember that the sprouts are alive and heat will kill them, so cover the pan to allow the tops of the eggs to finish cooking, or turn the eggs over and turn off the heat. Since the sprouts take no time to heat, we prefer to add them just before serving.

SPROUTED WHEAT BREAD is available in most supermarkets, and can be found in health food specialty stores.

DAY EIGHT

MENU: *Hot Corn Cereal*

Soft Boiled Egg

Sliced Melon

Pero, or other Coffee Substitute

---

4. You can sour milk by adding cider vinegar to it before blending it into the batter. Or, use fresh buttermilk. Another possible substitute is yogurt.

HOT CORN CEREAL

Mix together:

1 1/3 cups water (or 2/3 cup water and 2/3 cup raw milk)
1/2 cup undegerminated cornmeal
1/4 t. sea salt
1 T. butter

Put over medium heat and simmer, stirring often to prevent lumpiness, until meal thickens like cream of wheat. Then add:

2 T. sunflower seeds
2 T. sesame seeds
2 T. raisins (dried without chemicals), or other dried fruit

Cover, turn off heat and let stand 10 minutes before eating. When ready to serve, stir in one soft boiled egg per person. Eat as is, or top with raw honey.

For a creamier consistency, soak cornmeal in the liquid overnight. Left-over cereal can be chilled, sliced and sauteed in butter for a snack or for tomorrow's breakfast.

DAY NINE

MENU: *Roman Meal Pancakes*

Fresh Melon

Raspberry Leaf Tea or Coffee Substitute

ROMAN MEAL PANCAKES
In a mixing bowl blend:

1/2 cup wheat germ
1/2 cup corn meal
1-3/4 cup Roman Meal Cereal (available in supermarkets)
1-3/4 cups raw milk (or powdered reconstituted)
2 t. low sodium baking powder
1-1/2 t. sea salt
2 fertile eggs
2 T. oil

Mix at medium high speed for 3 to 5 minutes. Then fry as you do griddle cakes. Serve with honey and butter, or maple

syrup, or honey-based jam, or homemade toppings like apple
sauce.
 For best texture, mix the batter the night before and let
stand.

DAY TEN

MENU: *American Omelet*

           Wheat Toast and Jam

           Fruit in Season

           Beverage

AMERICAN OMELET

           1 tomato, red or green, cut in wedges
           1 green pepper, diced
           1/4 onion, diced (or chives, or green onions,
           diced)
           1/3 cup cheddar cheese, grated
           1/4 cup raw milk (or reconstituted powdered)
           4 eggs

 Heat oil in skillet. Sautee the vegetables until they just
begin to lose their shape. Mix milk and eggs and beat until
fluffy. Add cheese and mix well. Pour egg mixture into pan with
vegetables, stir, and cook. Before serving, top with sprouts
and/or wheat germ nuggets. Serves 3.

DAY ELEVEN

MENU: *Waffles with Cinnamon Honey*

           Sliced Melon or Cinnamon Oranges

           Alfalfa-Mint Herb Tea or Coffee Substitute

WAFFLES WITH CINNAMON HONEY

           Sour milk or buttermilk
           3 fertile eggs
           1-1/2 cup raw honey (optional)[5]

---

5. If you include honey in the batter, the waffles will be sweet
   enough to eat with only butter on top.

1 t. soda (optional, not recommended)
1 cup whole wheat flour
1/4 cup soy flour
1/4 cup wheat germ
1/4 cup food yeast or fragilis
2 t. low sodium baking powder
1/2 t. sea salt.
1 t. cinnamon
1/4 t. nutmeg
1/2 cup oil
1/2 cup sunflower seeds
1/2 cup raw nuts, chopped

Separate the eggs and beat the egg whites until stiff. Set aside. Mix and beat the other ingredients, except the seeds and the nuts. When batter is well beaten, fold in the nuts, seeds, and egg whites.

Bake in waffle iron as usual. Top with honey, cinnamon honey, honey and molasses, honey jam, or homemade topping like applesauce or peach preserves.

FOR VARIETY: add dried apple slices or other dried fruit.

DAY TWELVE

MENU: *Rolled Oats and Steamed Wheat*

Honey and Molasses

Natural Cheddar Cheese Sliced (or milk)

Fruit in Season

Peppermint Herb Tea, or Coffee Substitute

ROLLED OATS

In saucepan place:

1-1/2 cups rolled oats
4-1/2 cups water
2 t. sea salt

Bring to low boil, stir and cover, simmering 20 minutes. Add 2/3 cup steamed wheat, and continue simmering until the oats are soft and the wheat warm. The non-instant oats will not become so mushy as the commercial instant brands, and will hold their shape.

In individual bowls put:

1 heaping T. honey
1/2 t. molasses (less if the taste has not been developed)

Add cereal and stir.

DAY THIRTEEN

MENU: *Sprouted Wheat Eggs*

               Whole Grain Toast

               Refried Beans

               Fresh fruit in Season

               Peppermint Herb Tea or Coffee Substitute

SPROUTED WHEAT EGGS

Fry eggs as usual, but before turning the egg over, drop a handful of sprouted wheat on top. Salt to taste. Either cover the pan until the egg yolk solidifies to your preference, or turn eggs and turn off the fire, to prevent ruining the living sprouts with too much heat.

REFRIED BEANS

Heat corn oil in heavy sauce pan. When oil is hot, add chili beans and cook over low heat, stirring occasionally, and adding more oil when necessary to prevent sticking. The longer they fry, the better they will be. For added flavor, add garlic powder and granulated onion.

DAY FOURTEEN

MENU: *Granola*

               Fruit in Season

               Herb Tea or Coffee Substitute

HOMEMADE GRANOLA (Make ahead of time and store)

1 cup wheat germ
1 cup pumpkin seeds
1 cup sesame seeds
1 cup sunflower seeds

1 cup soy powder or milk
1 cup almonds, chopped
1 cup walnuts, or cashews, chopped
1/2 cup millet
1 cup rolled triticali
4 cups rolled oats
1 cup oil
1 cup raw honey
1/2 cup molasses
1 cup unsweetened coconut

Mix all the dry ingredients together. Add oil and honey and stir. Place on cookie sheets and bake in a slow oven (200 degrees, or less, if you have time) until granola browns. Stir occasionally. Remember that honey can burn easily. When done, add dried fruits of your choice, and remove from sheets and let cool before putting into a container. Granola makes a good snack food.

DAY FIFTEEN

MENU: *Cheddar Poached Egg*

Fresh Apricots or Fruit in Season

Alfalfa-Mint Tea or Coffee Substitute

Poach eggs as usual, except for topping them with shredded cheddar cheese or grated Parmesan cheese.

DAY SIXTEEN

MENU: *Huevos Rancheros*

Fruit in Season

Beverage

HUEVOS RANCHEROS

In skillet fry two corn tortillas per person in corn oil. Drain, salt and set aside.
Cut into bite-size pieces:

1 tomato
1 green pepper
1/2 onion

Cover bottom of sauce pan with corn oil. When oil is hot, add vegetables, plus:

> 2 t. honegar
> 1 to 2 t. chili pepper or cayenne (according to taste)

Heat slowly, just until vegetables begin to lose their shape. Leave uncovered and stir often. Keep warm while you fry two eggs per person.

To serve, place two tortillas on each plate, top with two eggs and cover with the sauce. Sauce recipe serves two persons.

LUNCHES

Most of us don't have much time to fix lunches, so we have not offered complicated or fancy ones. In most cases we haven't included a full menu, since a sandwich or soup plus a beverage is usually sufficient. You will want to use whatever juice or beverage you have on hand. We assume that you will want to include fresh fruit and a salad whenever possible.

Some of the fruit desserts presented with the dinners would make very good lunch food, and some of the lunches will make full-fledged dinners.

SALADS TO CHOOSE FROM

Fresh Fruit
Waldorf Cabbage
Sliced Tomatoes and Onions
Apricot-nut or Peach-nut
Banana-Orange Coconut
Lemon-Green Salad

BREADS TO CHOOSE FROM

Banana Nut
Grapenut
Graham nut
Roman Meal Muffins
Cheese Muffins
Peanut Bread
Gingerbread
Corn Bread
Spoon Bread

QUICK SANDWICHES

Tuna Sprout
Pumpkin Peanut Butter

Sardine
Peanut Butter Banana
Egg
Tamales
Allburgers
Open-Faced Egg Salad
Grilled Sprout-Cheese
Tomato, Avocado, Sprout
Olive nut

TUNA SPROUT

Mix one can drained tuna with mayonnaise, honegar, wheat sprouts, or alfalfa sprouts, or both, 1 T. finely chopped onion, some chopped green pepper and cucumber and a touch of wheat germ, and serve with fresh green spinach in place of lettuce between whole grain or soy bread. Slices of tomato are good too.

PUMPKIN PEANUT BUTTER

On a piece of whole wheat toast spread very lightly raw honey (optional), top with raw or sunroasted peanut butter, and cover with a handful of raw pumpkin seeds. We suggest milk or buttermilk or yogurt and fruit to go with it to obtain a satisfactory protein complement.

SARDINE

Spread a piece of whole wheat toast with mayonnaise, cover with a layer of canned sardines, thinly sliced onion, tomato slices (in season), very thinly sliced dill pickle, spinach or lettuce leaves, and cover with another toasted slice of wheat bread that has been lightly spread with mustard. Good with apple juice or unsweetened grape juice.

BANANA PEANUT BUTTER

Spread soy bread with raw or sun roasted peanut butter, wheat sprouts, sesame seeds and sliced bananas. Dribble raw honey over top, and cover with another slice of soy bread. Serve with buttermilk or protein drink.

EGG SANDWICHES

In frying pan melt butter and slowly fry eggs, topped with thin slices, or grated, cheddar or monterrey jack cheese. Salt to taste. Don't turn the eggs; instead cover them and cook slowly. Serve on whole wheat toast and spread with mayonnaise. For extra value add mung sprouts or alfalfa sprouts and/or lettuce or spinach leaves. Serve with apple or grape juice.

GRILLED SPROUT CHEESE SANDWICH

For each sandwich use 2 slices of sprouted wheat bread and spread with mayonnaise. Add:

> sliced cheddar cheese
> alfalfa or mung bean sprouts
> pumpkin seeds

Butter the outside of the sandwich and grill slowly. Serve with a fruit salad.

OPEN-FACED EGG SALAD SANDWICH

Mix together with mayonnaise and honegar:

> 1 hard boiled egg, chopped
> chopped onion, to taste
> alfalfa sprouts
> sunflower seeds

On slice of whole grain bread place lettuce (or spinach), tomato, and egg salad. Makes one.

TOMATO-AVOCADO-SPROUT SANDWICH

On slice of whole-grain bread place:

> sliced tomato
> sliced avocado
> alfalfa sprouts
> Vegesal and pepper to taste
> kelp
> raw pumpkin seeds
> mayonnaise or blue cheese dressing (see recipe)

Top with another slice of bread. Serve with orange spa and waldorf cabbage salad.

OLIVE NUT

Be careful when buying olives to make sure they don't contain preservatives or artificial coloring. Good ones can usually be found in specialty food shops like delicatessens, and Italian Specialty Foods. Often they are found in the meat case.

> 1/4 pound green olives, pitted, drained and chopped
> 1/3 cup walnuts, chopped
> 3/4 cup mayonnaise salad dressing[6]

Mix together and serve open-face on wheat toast.

TAMALES

Read the label before buying, to make sure no sugar, starches, or artificial additives are included. Heat according to package directions. Top with raw tomato relish, and serve with apple juice.

FRESH FRUIT SALAD

Cut into bite-size pieces

> watermelon
> cantaloupe
> honeydew
> fresh peaches
> green grapes

Mix together, sprinkle with lime juice and drizzle lightly with honey. Let stand about an hour to allow honey to cover all the fruit.

WALDORF CABBAGE SALAD

Mix together:

> 1/4 head fresh cabbage, grated or shredded
> 4 oz. fresh mushrooms, sliced
> 1 small onion, sliced
> 1 tart apple, cored and sliced
> 1/8 cup wheat sprouts
> 1/4 cup alfalfa sprouts

---

6. For extra flavor whenever you use mayonnaise, add 1 t. honegar to each ½ c mayonnaise.

1/4 cup walnuts, chopped
1-1/4 cups mayonnaise mixed with honegar

Add salt, pepper and granulated kelp to taste. Place in serving dish and top with fresh tarragon and paprika.

SLICED TOMATOES AND ONIONS

Slice tomatoes, sprinkle with chopped onions, and serve with dash of sea salt, cider vinegar and sunflower, safflower, or soy oil, or olive oil over top.

APRICOT-NUT SALAD

Cut in half and pit 12 fresh apricots. Add:

1/8 cup slivered raw almonds
1/8 cup chopped raw pecans or walnuts

Sprinkle with juice of a quarter of a lemon. Add 1 T. honey and a dash of cinnamon. Mix together.
Peaches can be substituted for the apricots.

BANANA-ORANGE SALAD

Peel and cut into bite-size pieces:

2 oranges
2 bananas

Mix together. Add:

1/8 cup unsweetened coconut
1/8 to 1/3 cup honey
1/8 cup chopped pecans or walnuts (optional)

Mix well, let stand at least one-half hour, and serve.

LEMON-GREEN SALAD

Break into edible size one package spinach leaves. Wash and dry, then chill. Mix together:

1/4 cup sliced green onions
3 T. lemon juice
3 T. olive oil
1/4 t. sea salt
1/8 t. dry mustard

Blend oil, lemon, salt, and mustard, and pour over spinach just before serving. This will make a large salad. To make a smaller amount, use your judgment in how much spinach to prepare.

TUNA SALAD

In bowl place greens of your choice, sunflower seeds, vegetables in season (preferably grated), and sprouts, and top with drained tuna. Sprinkle top with cider vinegar and sunflower, safflower, soy or olive oil, and salt, pepper, paprika, and granulated kelp to taste. Serve with apple juice, grape juice or pineapple spa, and banana nut bread.

RAW VEGETABLE PLATE

Wash and cut into bite-size, edible pieces:

> fresh mushrooms
> fresh green onions
> tomatoes
> radishes
> celery
> zucchini
> cucumbers
> carrots

Serve chilled on a leaf-lettuce bed. Top with this dip, or serve dip for vegetables to be dipped into:

> 1/3 cup bleu cheese
> 1/3 cup mayonnaise
> 1/3 cup yogurt
> dash fresh lemon juice
> dash sea salt to taste (or kelp)

If you chill the plate before serving, be sure the food is covered to prevent vitamin loss to the air
Serve with cheese muffins.

ALLBURGERS

These are especially handy for picnics, and they contain all the seasoning you will want.
Take the normal amount of hamburger you would use for a patty, and divide it into two patties. On one of the patties spread

mustard, legal ketchup, other sauces as desired, salt and pepper and kelp to taste, and top with onion slices and natural cheese. Put second patty over top and seal the edges. You have an allburger. No need to serve condiments with them because they are all inside, seasoning the meat as it cooks. This is great for outdoor cooking, since it eliminates all those extras to be carried out, and then back into the house.

Good served with home-made French Fried Onion Rings (in olive oil) made with our basic batter, and carob pudding.

CAROB PUDDING

Cook 3 eggs in 1 cup water. First break the eggs into a small bowl, and whip with fork while water is heating. As soon as the water is simmering, stir the eggs into it, and continue to stir until the eggs begin to thicken. They should be removed from the heat and put into the blender before they begin to solidify. They will be the consistency of a cream filling before it has cooled.

With the blender running, add the water and egg mixture and:

> 1/4 cup honey
> 1/2 cup oil
> 2-1/2 T. carob
> 1 t. pure vanilla

It may be served warm, or chilled first. It may be frozen for fudgesicles or used for hot chocolate base. It can be put into small sherbet glasses and topped with a sprinkle of unsweetened coconut, or a dab of homemade marshmallow. Tell company it is chocolate mousse, or double the recipe and use as a carob fudge pie filling.

LUNCH

MENU: *Spanish Tortilla*

Lemon-Green Salad

Garlic Bread

Sliced melon, honeydew if available

SPANISH TORTILLA

When you say *tortilla* in Spain, you aren't referring to the flat corn cake of Mexico, but to an omelet. The tortilla francesa

is a simple, plain egg omelet. The *tortilla espanola* is a large pan-size egg *cake* mixed with potatoes and onions, and it is delicious cold for picnics and for sandwich filling. It is a good way to use up cooked potatoes.
Sautee in olive oil:

> 4 cups cooked potatoes
> 2 onions, diced

In a bowl beat 5 to 8 eggs. Add the potato and onions and stir. Pour mixture back into hot fry pan that is well oiled with olive oil. Cook slowly, covered, over low heat. When the eggs seem to be set on the bottom, and fairly well on the top, remove skillet from heat, place large dinner plate upside down on top of skillet, and tip the fry pan upside down so that the contents fall onto the right side of the plate. Then slide the omelet back into the fry pan. This allows you to cook the top, which is not on the bottom. Turn off the heat, leave uncovered, and let the residual heat finish cooking the eggs. When eggs are solid, cut like a pie and serve, or allow to cool before cutting and serving, depending on how you want to eat it.

GARLIC BREAD

Spread whole grain bread with this garlic butter, then toast under broiler.
Melt together:

> 1/4 cup butter
> 3 cloves garlic, crushed

Top with sprinkle of paprika, Parmesan cheese, and parsley flakes. Or spread butter on bread, sprinkle with garlic powder as well as above condiments, and broil until lightly toasted and butter is melted.

LUNCH

MENU: *Frijoles Negros con Arroz*
(Black Beans with Rice)

Sliced Melon

Green Lettuce-Vegetable Salad

FRIJOLES NEGROS CON ARROZ

Black beans with rice is a typical dish of the South American countries, particularly Brazil. It is tasty and very filling, and there will be leftovers for another meal (or they can be frozen). Plan ahead about three days for these beans. Soak 2 cups of black turtle beans overnight. Drain and save the stock. Sprout the beans. In about two days when the sprout is as long as the bean, they are ready to be cooked.

Place beans in heavy cooking kettle and cover with the sprouting stock and other vegetable stock to cover. Add:

> 2 large onions, sliced or diced
> 3 bay leaves
> 6 cloves garlic, chopped or crushed
> 1/2 small can tomato sauce
> 1 can whole tomatoes
> 1/2 cup red wine or 1/3 cup cider vinegar
> 1 t. each raw honey and molasses

Cover and simmer until beans are soft. Salt to taste. Serve over brown rice. Top beans with marinated onions and *farafa*. This will give you a full protein complement as well as an authentic Latin dish.

MARINATED ONIONS

Marinate in a covered bowl at least two days:

> 1 onion, chopped
> 1/2 cup cider vinegar
> 1/2 cup water
> 1 t. sea salt

FARAFA

Toast ground cornmeal over low heat in corn oil until meal browns slightly. Watch it carefully to prevent burning.

LUNCH

MENU: *Hunza-Style Potato Soup*

Sliced Cucumber with Vegesal and Fresh Ground Pepper

Garlic Butter Toast

French Omelet (optional)

HUNZA STYLE POTATO SOUP

2 medium potatoes
2 small carrots
1 small onion

Grate or slice thinly the potatoes and carrots. Place in sauce pan, barely cover with water, and simmer about 5 minutes to tenderize. Pour contents into blender, add dab of butter, vegesal, and pepper to taste. For extra zest add fresh dill. Serve immediately with dollup of yogurt.

GARLIC BUTTER TOAST

Toast whole grain soy bread and spread with this basic butter:

BASIC BUTTER

Soften one pound butter. In blender or with electric mixer beat into the butter:

1-1/2 t. garlic powder
1 cup olive oil
1/2 t. rosemary

Put into container and refrigerate for future use.

FRENCH OMELET

Potatoes should have the addition of some dairy product to increase the usable protein of the potato. We suggest adding powdered milk or egg to the soup while in the blender, or using the yogurt on top, drinking milk with the soup, or fixing a quick omelet.

Whip together:

2 eggs
1 T. milk

In fry pan warm butter or olive oil to cover bottom. Add the eggs. When the eggs appear solid, fold over one half the omelet so that you have a half-moon-shaped omelet. Continue to cook very slowly over low heat until center of omelet is done.
Serves one as a main dish, or two as a side dish.

LUNCH

MENU: *Chili Beans with Relish*

              Corn Bread

              Green Vegetable Salad

              Apple Juice

CHILI BEANS

Soak 4 cups of beans overnight. Use pinto, pink, red or any similar type bean. Drain and save stock. Sprout the beans. When sprout is same length as the bean they are ready to cook. Put into kettle and cover with stock, including your soak water. Add:

> 1 large onion, diced
> 4 cloves garlic, crushed
> 1 large can whole tomatoes
> 1 medium can tomato sauce
> 3 bay leaves
> 1 T. dry mustard or 2 T. prepared mustard
> dash soy sauce
> dash Worchestershire sauce (optional)
> 1/4 cup honegar
> 1 t. molasses (more for more brown sugar effect)
> 2 t. cayenne
> chili pepper and sea salt to taste

Simmer until tender about four hours.

LUNCH

MENU: *Berry Waffles with Yogurt*

              Iced Pero or Peppermint Tea

BERRY WAFFLES

Make basic waffles (recipe in breakfast section.) Mix honey with fresh berries in season and let stand, covered, ½ hour. When waffles are ready, cover with berries, and top with yogurt and chopped raw almonds.

SOUPS

Pumpkin Soup
Split Pea Soup

Leek Soup
Quick Vegetable Soup
Summer Soup
Lentil Soup

PUMPKIN SOUP

Place 3 cups cooked pumpkin in 3 cups scalded raw (or reconstituted powdered) milk. Add:

1 T. butter
1 T. raw honey
1 T. molasses
sea salt to taste
pumpkin pie spice to taste
pinch of saffron

Simmer, covered, until warm. Add pepper and serve at once.

Pumpkin is very similar in flavor to squash, though milder than the acorn squash most of us are used to. It is highly nutritious and very inexpensive, and seems to have been a favorite with Mexicans for centuries. This soup is very rich, and if your family likes milk, they will like this soup.

Serve with wheat sesame baking powder biscuits (see breads) and honey.

For dessert baked apple slices would be good.

COOKING PUMPKIN

Cut pumpkin into pieces that will fit into your steamer or on a baking sheet. Wash, drain, and dry seeds. (They can be salted and eaten as snacks. They are high in zinc, a so-called fertility mineral.)

Steam pumpkin over water, or place pumpkin pieces, skin side up, on baking sheet with water covering the surface of the sheet. Bake in slow oven (not over 180 degrees) until pumpkin is tender. Remove pumpkin from skins and use immediately, or freeze. For a creamier consistency, we recommend blending the pumpkin.

LEEK SOUP

6 leeks
1 or 2 potatoes
1 quart water

2 T. butter
1 T. cornstarch or arrowroot
2 T. parsley, chopped

Wash, but do not peel leeks and potatoes. Dice or grate and brown them lightly in butter. Add water and simmer until tender. Blend in blender. Then reheat, adding arrowroot to thicken. Serve with chopped parsley on top, and with gingerbread.

LENTIL SOUP

Soak overnight:

1 cup green lentils

Drain lentils. In 4 cups simmering water add:

1 medium onion, sliced
1 clove garlic, sliced
2 stalks celery, chopped
1 carrot, chopped
1 bay leaf
1/2 t. sea salt

Simmer, covered for 45 minutes. When ready to serve, add one or two tablespoons of fresh lemon juice, and (optional) a spoonful of yogurt for each serving. Serve with grapenut bread.

SPLIT PEA SOUP

Wash 1 cup split peas. Soak in 4 cups water for 30 minutes (or in stock for a stronger flavor and more nutritious soup). Add:

1 medium onion, chopped
1 clove garlic, chopped
1 carrot, grated
1 stalk celery, grated
1 bay leaf
1/2 t. sea salt

Simmer slowly 30 minutes, covered. Add 1 T. each of butter and oil and simmer another 30 minutes. To make smooth, blend in blender or mash with potato masher. Add 1 cup whole raw milk. Warm thoroughly and serve with wheat croutons lightly toasted in a skillet in butter, granulated onion, garlic powder, vegesal and/or Spike. Serve with Roman Meal Muffins.

ST. JOHN'S BROWNIES

Melt together:

> 1/2 cup carob
> 1/2 cup butter

Add:

> 2/3 cup whole wheat flour, or wheat and soy flour, half-and-half
> 1 cup honey
> 2 eggs

Beat well, and then add:

> 3/4 cup whole wheat flour or soy-wheat combination
> 2/3 cup nuts, chopped
> 1 t. pure vanilla

Bake one-half hour at 325 degrees. Cut into squares while hot and sprinkle date sugar on top or leave plain.

SUMMER SOUP

In blender put:

> 4 medium zucchini, sliced
> 1 stalk celery
> 1 medium onion, grated
> 1 small potato, raw and grated

Cover with stock and blend until pureed. Pour into saucepan, and heat slowly until warm. Before serving add:

> 1 t. vegesal or
> 1 t. vegetable broth seasoning
> 1 t. Spike
> 1 T. butter

Serve with dollup of yogurt on top.

This soup tastes best when the vegetables are as raw as possible, so be careful not to overcook.

Serve with Peanut Bread.

QUICK VEGETABLE SOUP

In soup pan brown in oil ground meat: beef, turkey, or lamb. When almost browned, add 1 large onion, diced, and as many grated fresh vegetables as you would like. Sautee slightly. Add stock to cover, or more if desired, salt, pepper, and garlic powder to taste. You may also want to add dashes of tarragon and thyme as well as a few bay leaves.

Simmer until the vegetables are almost done. Since they are grated they will cook quickly, and they should remain slightly crunchy. Five minutes before you are ready to eat, add strips of natural cheese over top. Cover and finish simmering until cheese is melted.

Serve with graham nut bread.

BREADS

BANANA NUT BREAD

Preheat oven to 300 degrees, or cook in a pan over boiling water. Blend:

> 1/3 cup safflower oil
> 2/3 cup raw honey
> 3/4 t. grated lemon rind

Beat in:

> 2 beaten, fertile eggs
> 4 to 6 ripe bananas

Add:

> 2 cups whole wheat flour
> 2-1/4 t. low sodium baking powder

When blended, stir in 1 cup nut meats. Pour into greased bread pan or steaming pan and bake or steam about one hour.

GRAPENUT BREAD

This is a tasty, sweet, rich-flavored bread. Soak one hour:

> 1/2 cup grapenuts
> 1 t. soda
> 7/8 cup sour milk

Add:

> 1 egg
> 1/2 cup honey
> 1 1/3 cups whole wheat flour
> 2 T. oil
> 1 t. sea salt

Beat well. Bake in small bread pan one hour at 350 degrees or steam over boiling water for one hour. You may wish to decorate top with whole walnuts.

GRAHAM CRACKER NUT BREAD

> 1 cup honey
> 1/3 cup oil
> 2 fertile eggs, beaten
> 2/3 cup milk
> 1 t. vanilla
> 2/3 cup whole wheat flour
> 1/2 t. sea salt
> 2/3 t. baking powder (low sodium)
> 1 cup nut meats

Blend honey and oil together. Add beaten eggs, then graham cracker crumbs. Combine milk with vanilla and add alternately with dry ingredients which have been sifted together. Finally, add nut meats. Put batter into loaf pan and bake in moderate oven for 40 minutes, or steam over boiling water for same length of time.

ROMAN MEAL MUFFINS

Preheat over to 400 degrees. Blend:

> 1 egg
> 3 T. honey
> 3 T. oil
> 1 cup raw milk

Add:

> 1/2 cup whole wheat flour
> 1/2 cup wheat germ
> 1 T. low sodium baking powder
> 1 t. sea salt
> 1 cup Roman Meal

Stir to moisten. Don't overmix. Fill well-greased muffin cups 2/3 full. Bake 20 to 25 minutes.

CHEESE MUFFINS

Mix together:

> 1 cup cornmeal
> 3/4 cup whole wheat flour
> 1/4 cup wheat germ
> 2 T. low-sodium baking powder
> 1/2 t. sea salt

Blend with:

> 3 T. raw honey
> 1 cup raw milk
> 1/4 cup oil

Fold in:

> 1 fertile egg, beaten
> 1 cup cheddar cheese, grated
> 1/3 cup nuts, chopped

Fill well-oiled muffin tins and bake at 375 degrees for 20 to 30 minutes, or steam over boiling water for same length of time.

PEANUT BREAD

> 1/2 cup soft butter
> 1/2 cup peanut butter[7]
> 1/4 cup unsulfured molasses
> 3 fertile eggs
> 1/2 cup raw honey
> 1 T. vanilla
> 1/2 cup buttermilk (or sour milk)
> 2 cups whole wheat flour
> 1 t. low sodium baking powder
> 1 t. soda (optional)
> 1/8 t. sea salt
> 1 T. food yeast

---

7. Make your own peanut butter. Roast raw peanuts all day in 170-degree oven. Put into blender and grind finely. Add just enough peanut oil to make the mixture spreadable.

In large mixing bowl beat together the butter, peanut butter, and molasses until blended. Add eggs one at a time and beat until fluffy. Stir in honey, vanilla, and buttermilk. Mix flour with baking powder, soda and salt and yeast. Add to cream mixture. Mix well. Spoon batter into a greased 9 by 5 inch loaf pan. Bake at 325 degrees for 55 minutes or until a wooden pick inserted in the center comes out clean. Let cool in pan for 10 minutes, turn out and cool completely. Makes one loaf. (May be steamed over boiling water for same length of time.)

If you buy peanut butter, be sure it is only nuts, oil and maybe salt. Most commercial brands have some form of sugar as well as chemicals added, besides being hydrogenated.

GINGERBREAD

1 1/3 cups whole wheat flour
1/4 cup raw honey
1 T. baking powder
2 t. each ground cinnamon and ginger
1/4 t. sea salt
1 fertile egg
1/2 cup molasses
1/3 cup oil
1/2 cup boiling water

In a bowl stir together the flour, honey, baking powder, cinnamon, ginger and salt. In another bowl beat together the egg, molasses and oil. Stir in the flour mixture until blended, then add the boiling water. Mix until blended.

Pour into greased and floured 8-1/2 by 4-1/2 inch loaf pan, and bake at 350 degrees for about 30 minutes. Cool in pan 10 minutes, then remove from pan and let cool on rack. Serve with honey butter sauce. (You may prefer to steambake the bread.)

HONEY-BUTTER SAUCE

1 cup honey
lump butter
3 to 4 T. arrowroot
2 cups water
2 T. vanilla

Mix together and cook until thick, like a cream filling for a pie. Serve warm or hot over the top of the gingerbread.

VARIATION: Cover bottom of gingerbread pan with honey and molasses, about 2/3 cup honey to 2 T. molasses. Arrange 1 large can drained, washed apricot halves, cut-side down in single layer over honey. Pour gingerbread mixture over this and bake. When done, immediately invert onto serving plate.

CORN BREAD

2 cups corn meal
1 t. sea salt
1/2 cup powdered milk
2 t. low sodium baking powder
2 T. honey
3 fertile eggs
1 cup milk, or sour milk, or buttermilk, or goat yogurt
1/2 cup wheat germ
2 T. oil or butter (butter gives richer and corny-er taste).

Separate eggs, and beat egg whites until stiff. Mix all other ingredients, and fold in the stiffened egg whites last. Pour into greased pan and top with wheat germ nuggets or chopped raw nuts. Bake at 400 degrees or bake over steaming water, until toothpick stuck into the center comes out clean. Serve with lots of butter.

SPOON BREAD

This is a very delicious "bread" and especially good with chili beans.

1/2 cup corn meal
1-1/3 cups raw milk (or reconstituted powdered)
3 eggs
1/4 t. sea salt
2 T. raw honey
3 T. butter

Mix together milk and cornmeal, heat slowly, stirring often, until they reach the consistency of corn meal mush.
Separate eggs. Beat egg whites until stiff and set aside.
When corn mush is ready, add egg yolks, sea salt, honey and butter. Fold in the egg whites, and pour into well-greased, 2-quart casserole dish. Bake at 350 degrees about 40 minutes. It will rise several inches above dish. Serve immediately after

removing from the oven, since, like souffles, it will fall as soon as cooler air hits it. (Don't peak in oven, either, or it will fall when you open the door.)

Can be served with honey, but is delicious with just butter, or plain.

BREAD[8]

We recommend making your own bread, or buying it at health food stores. There are some brands available in supermarkets that are all right too. Just be sure to read the labels.

There are many, many recipes and directions and hints for making bread and we won't take time to go into them here. In fact, there are whole cookbooks in paperback that deal just with breads. We have included one basic whole wheat bread recipe so it is handy and available to you.

JEAN'S WHOLE WHEAT BREAD

In 5 cups warm water, dissolve 2 T. yeast. As soon as it is activated, add:

> 2 T. sea salt
> 1/3 cup safflower oil
> 1 cup raw honey (you may wish to mix some molasses with the honey.)

Mix together and add about 14 cups flour. You want a consistency that can be kneaded with your hands without the dough sticking to them. If you need more flour, use it. You can't knead dough if it is sticking to your hands like a huge mitten.

To knead, either flour a board or pastry cloth, or flour your formica counter, or oil the counter. See a basic cookbook for pictures on how to knead. Basically what you are doing is working the gluten of the flour to develop it. You could pound it

---

8. . . . If you are going to eat bread. Even whole grain breads are not very healthy, since the grains have a very high pH factor, because they are baked at high temperatures. This makes bread a mucous-forming food, and the less mucous in our bodies, the healthier we will be.

with a wooden mallat or whatever, to develop this gluten. Most people simply work it by pushing the dough away from them with the heels of the hands, and then pulling it towards them, over and over again. You can tell when the gluten is developed because the dough becomes satiny and very elastic.

When gluten is developed, put dough into greased dish, swirl around to get all sides of dough greased, and let rise until double in size. To test it, stick two fingers into dough. If imprint remains, the dough has risen enough.

Once the dough has reached double its size, knead again, and divide into four parts, Make into loaves and place in four greased loaf pans, let rise again, but not until double. Bake at 350 degrees until done.

OR use one part for dinner rolls.

WHOLE WHEAT DANISH

Mix:

> 3-1/2 cups warm water
> 6 T. yeast
> 1 cup corn or soy oil
> 1/2 cup raw honey

Let stand 15 minutes. Add:

> 3 fertile eggs
> 2 T. sea salt
> 10-1/2 cups whole grain flour

Mix for 10 minutes in bread mixer, or knead well by hand.

Cut dough in half. Roll out each half into an oblong as thinly as possible (1/2 inch approximately).

Spread generously with butter and raw honey. Sprinkle with 1 cup chopped nuts and cinnamon to taste.

Roll as for jelly roll.

Cut into 1 inch slices. Place spiral side up on well-buttered cookie sheet. Let rise 10 minutes. Bake 10 minutes at 425 degrees.

VARIATION: Spread honey-sweetened preserves on top before baking. Peach and apricot are especially good. Add raisins before rolling up the dough.

VARIATION: Use basic dough recipe and form hamburger buns. Bake as above.

SOME BREAD HINTS

1. *Keep the dough soft and pliable. Add the flour gradually so that the dough is no stiffer than necessary, and can be handled easily.*
2. *When using raw milk, be sure to heat it to simmering to destroy molds and bacteria that might interfere with the yeast.*
3. *Use of water in whole wheat bread brings out the flavor of the grain more than milk will.*
4. *Thorough kneading is a must to bring together the particles of gluten which makes for elasticity and good texture.*
5. *There are electric mixers that are especially designed to knead bread.*
6. *A beaten egg will promote the action of the yeast and make the bread lighter textured.*

DINNERS

DAY ONE

MENU: *Rouladen*

   Mashed Potatoes

   Buttered Steamed Carrots and Parsnips

   Sunshine Salad

   Strawberry Shortcake

ROULADEN

Essentially rouladen are thin pieces of meat rolled up and stuffed. You may buy flank steak from the meat counter and make one big roll, though we find that individual rouladen is tastier. Ask the butcher to cut the flank steak very thin.

   2-1/2 pounds flank steak, sliced thinly
   1 large dill pickle, sliced into rings or diced
   1/4 pound fresh mushrooms, sliced
   1 small onion, diced
   1/4 cup wheat sprouts
   1/4 cup nut meats, chopped (optional)

Cut meat into 8 pieces. Brush one side with butter or olive oil, mustard, steak sauce and soy sauce. Season with sea salt and garlic powder. Mix together above ingredients, and drop mixture onto each piece of meat. Roll the meat around the mixture and tie the "log" with string, or secure with poultry nails. Place these rouladen in a hot oiled skillet and brown. Turn heat down to simmer, cover and let cook through—about 3 hours. If you are not using stainless cookware, you will need to add some liquid which can be stock or red wine. Pour 1/2 cup liquid over meat before covering to simmer. Add pepper when cooking is finished, before serving. Left-over mixture makes good pre-dinner snacking. Serves four.

CARROTS AND PARSNIPS

2 medium carrots
2 medium parsnips

Wash vegetables, but don't peel. Cut into rounds, steam and sautee in the butter. Season with butter, vegesal and sea salt when done, OR: grate vegetables. Melt 1 T. butter in pan, add vegetables, season with sea salt and vegesal and cover. Warm slowly.

STRAWBERRY SHORTCAKE

Wash and cut up strawberries as usual. For each cup used, add 1/3 cup honey. Stir, chill and allow to stand at least 1 hour. Use left-over juice in lemonade.

SHORTCAKE

1 cup triticali flour
1 cup soy flour
1 t. salt
2-1/2 t. low sodium baking powder
6 T. butter
1 cup raw milk

Cut butter into dry ingredients. Add milk. Let stand 5 minutes, before spooning onto greased baking dish. Bake at 350 degrees for 40 to 45 minutes.

MASHED POTATOES

Steam 4 unpeeled medium potatoes until cooked through. Put potatoes into mixing bowl, and add:

1 t. sea salt
2 T. Parmesan Cheese

pinch garlic powder
pinch onion powder (or granulated onion)
Spike or Salad Supreme
2 T. butter
fresh parsley, chopped, or parsley flakes

Whip at high speed, adding enough milk to make smooth. For extra nutrition add sprouts. Serve topped with paprika.

SUNSHINE SALAD

Wash, dry and break into edible size pieces redleaf and romaine lettuces for the number of people to be servedm Add:

1 can unsweetened pineapple chunks, drained
1/2 cucumber, sliced
1 can Mandarin orange slices, drained and rinsed, or
1 fresh orannge, sliced

Put fruit and cucumbers on top of lettuce leaves. Cover with Catalina dressing.

CATALINA DRESSING

1 cup oil
1/2 cup raw honey
1/2 t. sea salt
1/3 cup chili sauce
1/2 T. cider vinegar
1/2 cup onion, finely chopped
1 T. Worchestershire sauce

Blend together.

DAY TWO

MENU: *Fish Teriyaki*

Brown Rice with Sesame Seed Salt

Cinnamon Carrots

Tomato Salad with Green Mayonnaise

FISH TERIYAKI

Marinate 1 lb. cut up turbot or other white fish for 2 to 3 hours in:

1/3 cup Tamari or Kikkoman soy sauce
1 T. sake or white wine or white wine vinegar
juice and rind of one lemon or lime

Bake in 180 degree oven in marinade, or drain and charcoal grill, brushing with soy oil. Fish is done when it can be flaked with a fork. Serves 2.

CINNAMON CARROTS

Wash, and thinly slice 2 large carrots, Steam. Before serving add:

1 T. butter
1 T. raw honey
1 t. cinnamon
1/2 t. sea salt

Stir and serve. (Parsley flakes on top add color and nutrition.)

GREEN MAYONNAISE

Blanch in boiling water for 2 minutes:

12 spinach leaves
12 watercress leaves (or beet greens)
8 springs parsley

Drain resulting stock and save. Put 2 T. of stock in blender and add to blender:

1/2 t. garlic powder
1 t. chervil leaves
1 t. dried tarragon leaves
all the blanched greens

Blend 30 seconds at high speed. Then add:

1 cup mayonnaise
1/4 cup water
2 T. safflower or olive oil
sea salt
pepper

Serve over sliced, fresh tomatoes on bed of redleaf lettuce leaves. Add chopped green onions and raw sunflower seeds.
We recommend washing the rice first to remove the excess starch clinging to the outside of the grains. We have been told

that it is the custom in Thailand to wash the rice at least 14 times before cooking it. We wash it until the water we drain off is no longer milky.

WASHING RICE

Place dry rice in quantity desired into large bowl. Fill bowl with lukewarm water to cover rice. Stir with hands until water is milky. Drain water off into sink through a strainer to catch any rice that might fall into the sink. Repeat process until water is no longer milky.

BROWN RICE

In heavy sauce pan put:

> 2 cups brown rice
> 3-3/4 cups stock
> 1 t. sea salt
> 1 T. butter (or oil)
> 1 t. cinnamon
> dash suffron[9]
> 1/2 onion, diced[10]
> 2 cloves garlic, sliced[11]

Bring to low boil, stir, cover, and turn heat back to keep rice simmering. Simmer until rice kernels are no longer crunchy, about one hour. Brown rice takes longer to cook than the white rice since it still contains the nutty germ.

Many commercial directions for preparing brown rice recommend 3 cups of stock per one cup of rice. We find this makes the rice too sticky. We use slightly less than double the amount of liquid as rice used. Don't be embarrassed if the rice is slightly sticky. Contrary to what most of us imagine, real Oriental rice is somewhat sticky, which makes it easier to eat with chop sticks.

SESAME SALT

Cover the bottom of a small sauce pan with sesame oil, or other oil. Add 1 cup sesame seeds, 1 t. sea salt, and stir over low

---

9, 10, 11. Optional, but good.

heat until seeds are toasted. Watch them closely so they don't burn, and so that the valuable nutrients are not lost.

It is a good idea to serve sesame salt with rice each time you serve rice, since they are a perfect protein complement to the rice, supplying the essential amino acids that the rice is deficient in.

DAY THREE

MENU: *B-B-Q Chicken*

          Buttered Mint Peas

          Mashed Potatoes

          Sunshine Salad

          Graham Cracker Pie

B-B-Q CHICKEN

Marinate cut-up fryer in salad dressing made in a Good Seasonings bottle, using cider vinegar, water and olive oil, plus:

    2 T. Salad Supreme
    1 t. sea salt
    3 cloves garlic, crushed
    juice and rind of 1/2 lemon or lime
    dash soy sauce
    dash kelp

Drain meat for at least 1/2 hour before cooking. To grill, brush with olive oil or garlic butter (recipe in Lunches). Salt to taste.

BUTTERED MINT PEAS

Remove peas from pod and wash. Steam until warm through, but still bright green in color. Place in serving dish, top with butter, sea salt and pepper, and 1 T. chopped mint. OR make mint sauce to pour over them:

MINT SAUCE: Add 1 T. mint flakes to 2/3 cup honegar, full strength, and let stand at least overnight.

If you are using frozen peas, find a brand that doesn't contain sugar, and don't add any water when cooking, unless you check them and they appear dry. In most cases they accumulate plenty of water in the freezing process, and as they thaw you will usually find much too much water in the pan. Save this for the stock jar.

GRAHAM CRACKER PIE

CRUST:

1 package whole wheat graham crackers, crumbed
1/2 cup butter, melted.

Add melted butter to crumbs along with a pinch of sea salt and cinnamon. Press into pie tin, saving a few crumbs for the top of the pie. Bake 10 minutes at 350 degrees.

FILLING: In mixing bowl pour 1-1/2 cups raw milk (or reconstituted powdered). Slowly beat into the milk 6 T. whole wheat flour or 7 T. arrowroot, one tablespoon at a time. Slowly add 3 egg yolks (whites will be used for meringue) and 3/4 cup raw honey. When mixed together, but not beaten, pour into saucepan or double boiler and heat, stirring constantly, until the filling thickens like pudding. Remove from heat and add:

1 T. butter
1 t. vanilla

Pour into pie crust.
MERINGUE: Preheat oven to 350 degrees.
Make sure that all utinsels are absolutely free of grease, and that there is not a trace of yolk in the whites.
Whip until frothy 3 egg whites that are at room temperature, or 75 degrees. Add 1/4 t. cream of tartar and whip until stiff but not dry. They should stand in peaks. Add 3 T. raw honey, beat to blend and cover top of pie with the meringue, being careful to seal the edges. Bake until meringue is browned on the peaks.

Honey tends to decrease the volume of the meringue. You may want to use more egg whites. Don't expect a high meringue.

NOTE for hypoglycemics: this is a very rich pie and your tolerance for it may be low. Eat it sparingly, testing your tolerance for it.

DAY FOUR

MENU: *Salmon Patties*

          Rice-Carrot Patties

Basque Vegetables

Green Salad

SALMON PATTIES

Mix together:

1 can salmon
1 T. prepared mustard
1 fertile egg
dash sea salt and kelp
1/4 cup wheat sprouts
corn meal, enough to give mixture proper
consistency to make into patties.

Brown patties over low heat in skillet with oil that covers the bottom of the pan. Serve with lemon, or soy sauce dribbled over top, or make a pickle-less tartar sauce using mayonnaise and honegar to taste.

RICE-CARROT PATTIES

2 cups cooked brown rice
1/2 cup grated carrots
2 t. sea salt
1 fertile egg
wheat germ
sesame seeds

Mix the rice, salt, and carrots and form into patties. Dip patties into beaten egg, then into wheat germ and sesame seeds. Brown on well-oiled griddle over low heat, or bake on oiled cookie sheet in 350 degree oven until brown.

MEDITERRANEAN VEGETABLES

Cut into bite-size pieces:

1 large tomato
1 green pepper
1 medium onion

Sautee in corn oil or olive oil until just warmed through. Vegetables should remain crisp. Remove from pan. Add:

1/2 t. basil
1/2 t. rosemary
sea salt

Dribble with honegar. (Honegar and seasonings can be added to pan during warming.)

DAY FIVE

MENU: *Spanish Rice*

Green Salad

Fresh Fruit with Sticks of Monterey Jack Cheese

SPANISH RICE

1/2 lb. beef heart, cubed

corrections for above

1/2 t. basil
1/2 t. rosemary

Cover with water and Add:

1 medium onion, sliced
2 wedges lemon, squeezed (include rind)
1 large clove garlic, chopped
2 bay leaves

Simmer 6 to 8 hours. Then add:

1 small can tomato paste
2 green peppers, diced
2 cups cooked brown rice
1 T. raw honey
1/2 t. Italian Seasoning (available at supermarkets)
1/2 t. rosemary
sea salt to taste

Simmer until all ingredients are warm.

FRESH FRUIT DESSERT

Cut up fresh, in-season fruits. Cover with this dressing:

1/4 cup mayonnaise
1/4 cup yogurt
1 t. fresh lemon juice
1/8 t. powdered ginger

Serve with sticks of Monterey Jack cheese.

DAY SIX

SWISS FONDUE

Swiss fondue is a perfect party meal for people who like long meals and good conversation.

Cut into inch-size pieces whatever beef you can afford. Chuck or pot roast works if it is first marinated in garlic milk for a couple hours. To do this, crush a couple cloves of garlic into milk and place in a shallow pan. Put meat into pan and allow to marinate. Be sure to drain the meat thoroughly before serving, allowing 15 to 30 minutes minimum. This is to prevent a mushy meat.

Fill the fondue pot with peanut, olive, or safflower oil to about 2 inches from the top, and heat oil on stove. Check to see that the fondue burner has fluid in it.

Make the sauces in advance, so flavors can develop. Serve the meat in individual dishes for each person. Plan on about 3/4 pound per person. You may wish to add a few pieces of chicken liver, or some lamb—combinations are good.

Serve sauces in small bowls and pass them around so each one can choose what he'd like to use as dips for his meat. Usually each person puts a spoonful of each sauce that he wants on his plate, so it's ready for dipping when he has fried his meat.

Each one cooks his own meat in the fondue pot, sticking the meat on the forked end of the fondue fork. When it is cooked to his taste, he removes the meat from the very hot fork, dips it into the sauce(s) he wants and eats it. There are fondue dishes made especially to hold the different sauces—they have dividers to keep the sauces from mixing.

Since it takes a while for the meat to cook, serve salad and bread with the meal—preferably dishes that can't get hot or cold. Sour dough bread is especially delicious, or serve our "Health Bread" with lots of butter.

End the meal with pumpkin pudding.

FONDUE SAUCES

GARLIC BUTTER

Soften 1/2 pound butter, add three crushed garlic cloves, blend well, add parsley flakes or diced fresh parsley, and let stand at least 8 hours. Overnight is best.

SOUR CREAM HORSERADISH

Blend together:

1/2 pint (1 cup) unflavored yogurt
2 t. dry horseradish or 11/2 T. wet horseradish
1/2 t. sea salt (to taste)
1/2 lemon—juice

Sprinkle generously with black pepper. Let stand at least 8 hours. Top with chopped chives before serving.

STEAK SAUCE

Use your favorite steak sauce, add some diced, sauteed fresh mushrooms. And let everyone think you made it from scratch. (Most commercial steak sauces have additives and sugar in them. Use your judgment.)

BAR-B-QUE SAUCE

Pick out your favorite sauce. If it is a commercial brand, read the label for ingredients and use your judgment. Or make one from:

1 cup tomato sauce
juice 1/2 lemon
molasses to taste
garlic powder to taste
granulated onion to taste
dash Worchestershire sauce
salt to taste

CURRY SAUCE

Mix together 1/2 cup mayonnaise with 2 t. curry powder and let stand at least 8 hours. Taste. If it is not strong enough, add more curry, and if it is too strong for you, add more mayonnaise.

HEALTH BREAD

Have all ingredients at about 75 degrees. Crumble and dissolve for about 10 minutes:

1 cake (1 T. or one package) yeast
1/4 cup water at about 85 degrees

Scald 2 cups raw milk and pour over 1 cup rolled oats. Add:

> 2 t. sea salt
> 1/4 cup oil
> 1/2 cup honey

Cool this mixture to 85 degrees and add the dissolved yeast, plus:

> 1 or 2 slightly beaten eggs
> 1/4 to 1/2 cup wheat germ
> 1 cup soy flour
> 2 cups whole wheat flour or rye flour
> 3 to 4 cups gluten or soy and gluten mixture flour

Knead, shape and proof, allowing bread to rise in mixing bowl once, and once in the baking pan. Bake at 325 degrees for about one hour.

With the last kneading you can add some wheat germ and brewers yeast.

PUMPKIN PUDDING

Mix on top of double boiler, or over slow heat until thick:

> 1-1/2 cup cooked pumpkin[12]
> 1-1/2 cups undiluted evaporated milk or rich cream
> 1/3 cup raw honey
> 1 t. sea salt
> 1 t. cinnamon
> 1/2 t. ginger
> 1/8 t. cloves
> 1/2 cup blackstrap molasses
> 3 slightly beaten eggs.

Cool slightly and add:

> 1 t. brewers yeast
> 1 t. vanilla
> 3/4 cup nuts, chopped

Serve topped with whipped cream, or serve plain.

---

12. See how to cook your own punpkin in the Lunch Section

DAY SEVEN

MENU: *Lebanese Lamb Chops*

Brown Rice with Curry

Beets and Greens

Pecan Pie

LEBANESE LAMB CHOPS

Use any cut lamb chops, for two. In stainless steel or glass pan, marinate for 3 hours in the following:

> juice and rind of one lemon (or lime)
> 3 cloves garlic, crushed

Drain chops 1/2 hour before cooking to improve meat texture. Either char-grill, brushing with olive oil, or sautee slowly in olive oil in heavy skillet on stove.

BROWN RICE WITH CURRY

Fix brown rice as previously described, adding one tablespoon curry powder to rice while cooking.

BEETS AND GREENS

Grate the beets and cut up the beet greens and stalks. Steam together until cooked but still crisp. Add honegar, sea salt, butter and pepper to taste. If less sweet taste is desired, sprinkle with wine vinegar or lemon rather than the honegar.

MARY'S PECAN PIE

Beat together:

> 3 eggs
> 1 cup raw honey

Add:

> 2/3 cup raw honey
> 1/3 cup molasses
> 1/4 cup melted butter
> 1 t. vanilla
> 1 cup chopped pecans

Pour into unbaked pie crust and bake at 375 degrees for 15 or 20 minutes, until it is as solid as molded jello when the pan is shaken, or until a fork inserted into the center comes out clean.

PIE CRUST

2/3 cup butter
11/2 cups very finely ground whole wheat flour
1 t. sea salt
6 to 8 T. cold water

Cut shortening into flour. Add salt, and then the water, a little at a time and mix. Pat the dough into the pie tin.

DAY EIGHT

MENU: *Spaghetti*

Garlic Bread

Spinach Salad

Sliced Fresh Melon with Fresh Lime

Apple Crisp

SPAGHETTI

Use your favorite recipe, substituting sea salt, honey and such for the "bad" ingredients, or:
Brown 1 lb. ground meat (turkey and lamb work fine, and most people can't taste the difference) in 1/4 cup olive oil. When brown add:

1/2 lb. mushrooms, sliced
1 large onion, chopped
4 cloves garlic, crushed
1 bunch chopped parsley
1 large can whole tomatoes
1 can tomato sauce
1/8 t. rosemary
1/4 t. oregano
1/4 t. basil
1/4 t. sage
1/2 t. Italian Seasoning (at supermarkets)
2 T. honegar
2 dashes tobasio

sea salt to taste
1/2 cup red wine (optional)

Let simmer, uncovered, for a few hours, until consistency you prefer. If you make this ahead of time and let it stand for a day or so, the flavor will work through it. Put sauce over whole wheat or vegetable spaghetti, available in most health food stores. Simmer the spaghetti until it is soft. Top sauce with Parmesan cheese. Note: The sauce will have to be super-seasoned to compete with the stronger flavor of non-white spaghetti.

SPINACH SALAD

In salad bowl place:

1/2 package fresh spinach leaves (washed, dried, and broken into bite-size pieces)
1/2 small onion, sliced thinly
1/4 lb. fresh mushrooms, sliced thinly (optional)
1/2 cup alfalfa sprouts

Dressing: In Good Seasonings jar put cider vinegar, water, and olive oil. Add:

2 T. Salad Supreme (at supermarket)
1 t. sea salt
2 t. Parmesan cheese

Shake well. Dress salad and serve immediately.

APPLE CRISP

Soak 1/4 cup grapenuts in 1/4 cup orange juice, or 1/4 cup soy grits in ¼ cup sweet cider. Wash 6 large red apples, slice but don't peel, and place one-half of the apples in an oiled casserole. Combine:

3/4 cup whole wheat flour
1/4 t. nutmeg
1/2 t. allspice
1 T. food yeast
5/8 T. raw honey
4 T. safflower oil
1/4 t. molasses

Add soaked nuts to crumb mixture along with 1/2 to one cup chopped nuts. Sprinkle the apples in the dish with cinnamon, juice of half a fresh lemon, apple pie spice (optional) and cover with nut mixture. Place remaining apples over top and repeat process. Bake at 350 degrees for 30 minutes or steam over water. Serve warm or cold with dollup of plain yogurt or thick raw cream on top.

OPTIONAL: This can also be used as a pie filling. Fix exactly the same, but put into a bottom crust and bake until done.

DAY NINE

MENU: *Liver for Liver-Haters*

Hash Browns

Broccoli

Spinach Salad

LIVER FOR LIVER-HATERS

One of the secrets of cooking tasty organ meats is lemon, one of the best seasonings there is for just about any food— vegetables, rice, potatoes, meats and fish. Use it liberally.

Marinate the liver in the juice of one lemon (or lime) for about one hour. Drain the liver at least 30 minutes before cooking to prevent a mushy texture. Mix:

1/4 cup soy flour
1/4 cup whole wheat flour
1 T. food yeast or fragilis
1/4 t. kelp
1/4 t. paprika
1/8 t. crushed thyme
1 t. sesame salt (if you have some on hand)
2 T. sesame seeds

In skillet saute sliced onions just until they begin to turn limp. Remove, drain and save. Dip liver into flour mixture and brown quickly. It will take only about three minutes to get the liver brown and crusty on the outside and tender, moist and medium-well on the inside, so don't begin frying until everyone is ready to sit down and eat. Often the strong flavor associated with liver comes from over-cooking.

Remove to serving platter, and cover with onions and serve.

HASH BROWNS

Grate or slice, and fry in olive oil precooked potatoes, skins and all. Shortly before they are done add generous amounts of diced or sliced onion and continue frying until onions just begin to go limp. Season with Spike, sea salt, and just before serving, pepper.

BROCCOLI

Wash broccoli and cut off tough bottoms of the stems. Steam over simmering water until barely tender when pricked with a fork. They should be bright green and somewhat crispy. Remove to serving dish. Sprinkle with fresh lemon or lime juice, and season with sea salt, butter and pepper.

DAY TEN

MENU: *Grilled Fish*

Brown Rice

Zucchini Squash

Basque Tomatoes

Vanilla Chiffon Cream

GRILLED FISH

Marinate one pound fresh or frozen halibut, turbot, or black cod for three hours in:

1 lemon or 2 limes, juice and rind
1 clove garlic, crushed
2 t. Tamari or Kikkoman soy sauce

Drain at least one-half hour before grilling. Char-broil on open grill, brushing with olive oil, OR in winter, sautee in olive oil until fish is flaky. Serve with lemon or lime wedges, or with soy sauce.

ZUCCHINI

Wash and slice into rounds. Steam over simmering water until soft. Put into serving dish and add butter, salt, pepper and a pinch of allspice.

BASQUE TOMATOES

Slice tomatoes on individual plates. Top with diced onion, and sprinkle with salt, pepper, cider vinegar and olive oil.

VANILLA CHIFFON CREAM

1 T. vegetable gelatin
1/4 cup raw honey
1/8 t. sea salt
2 fertile eggs, separated
1-3/4 cups raw milk
1 1/2 t. vanilla

Mix gelatin, honey, salt, beaten egg yolks, milk and heat slowly, stirring constantly until gelatin dissolves and thickens. Remove from heat and stir in vanilla. Chill, stirring occasionally until thickened. Beat egg whites until they form soft peaks. Add 1 T. honey to eggs and beat again until stiff. Fold gelatin mixture into egg whites. Turn into oiled mold or individual dishes. Chill until set.

FOR LEMON CHIFFON: add 2 t. grated lemon rind and 2 T. lemon juice in place of vanilla.

DAY ELEVEN

MENU: *Arroz con Pollo (Chicken and Rice)*

Green and Red Salad

Peach Melba

ARROZ CON POLLO
CHICKEN AND RICE

Cut up left-over chicken into bite-size pieces. Over medium heat sautee in olive oil along with:

1/2 cup chopped onion
3 cloves fresh garlic, chopped

Add 2 to 3 cups cooked rice (as preferred). Salt to taste and heat, stirring occasionally, until rice is warmed through. Serve with lemon wedges to be squeezed over the rice.

GREEN AND RED SALAD

Cut into chunks:

2 fresh tomatoes
2 fresh green peppers
1 onion
4 large raw mushrooms

Dress with oil, cider vinegar, salt and pepper, and top with sesame seeds.

PEACH MELBA

Slice 2 fresh peaches and 2 fresh apricots (optional). Add 1/2 cup pecan or walnut meats, chopped and 2 T. wheat germ nuggets. Mix with 1 T. raw honey and a drop of molasses. Top with unsweetened shredded coconut. Let stand half an hour before serving to allow syrup to form.

DAY TWELVE

MENU: *Teriyaki Shish-Kabob*

Potato Salad (in winter, German Potato Salad)

Corn on the Cob

Whipped Orange-Peach Dessert

TERIYAKI SHISH-KABOB

Cut 1/2 lb. beef per person into thin strips or small cubes and marinate 12 to 24 hours in:

1 cup unsweetened pineapple juice
1/2 cup Tamari or Kikkoman soy sauce
2 cloves garlic, minced
1-1/2 t. ground ginger
1/4 to 1/2 cup sake, white wine or white wine vinegar.

The last hour of marinating add the pineapple chunks to the marinade. Let the meat drain for at least 30 minutes to prevent a disagreeable texture. Skewer meat and pineapple alternately with fresh vegetables cut into bite-size pieces, such as onion, green pepper, marinated mushrooms and cherry tomatoes. (Marinate mushrooms in honegar and salt.)
Lamb can be substituted for beef.

POTATO SALAD

Into bowl slice:

6 cooked potatoes, skins included
2 boiled eggs
1 small onion, diced
2 stalks celery, diced
8 radishes
1/3 cup alfalfa sprouts
1/3 cup wheat sprouts
1/3 cup fresh raw mushrooms
1 green pepper

Dressing:

11/2 cups mayonnaise
1 T. honegar
1 T. parsley flakes or
3 T. fresh parsley, chopped
2 T. wheat germ
1 t. celery seed (or dill seed)

Season with sea salt, pepper, granulated kelp, paprika, Spike and vegesal. Add dressing to potatoes, stir, and top with paprika and chopped parsley.

Parsley is high in minerals, so use it wherever possible.

Eggs and wheat germ complement the EAAs of the potato to give you more usable protein.

DAY THIRTEEN

MENU: *Tuna-Avocado Salad*

Artichoke

Herb Popovers

Apple Betty

TUNA-AVOCADO SALAD
A summer dish

In each individual salad bowl place romaine and iceberg lettuces that have been washed, dried and chilled. Add:

1/2 can tuna, drained
1 small avocado, sliced
4 green onions, sliced
1 handful alfalfa sprouts
raw mushrooms, sliced

Squeeze a large wedge of fresh lemon over the bowl. Add sea salt and pepper to taste. Top with dressing of your choice. Top with oil and vinegar or green goddess dressing. (Include tomato wedges when tomatoes are in season.)

GREEN GODDESS DRESSING

3/4 cup mayonnaise
3 T. raw milk or yogurt
2 anchovies, minced
1 T. vinegar
1-1/2 t. lemon juice
1 cup parsley sprigs, minced
2 T. chives, finely chopped

Mix together. Makes one cup

ARTICHOKE

With scissors cut off spiny ends of each leaf. With knife cut off remaining "thorns" at top of artichoke. Wash. Steam 4 to 6 hours over simmering water to which you have added:

3 bay leaves
3 cloves garlic
1/4 cup cider vinegar or red wine

Test for doneness by pulling off an outer leaf. When it nearly falls off and the bottom near the stem is soft and easily eaten off the leaf it is cooked enough. Serve with dip of:

1 cup mayonnaise mixed with 1 T. honegar
1 t. sea salt
1 t. Spike (at supermarkets)

Serve artichoke whole. Eat one leaf at a time, dipping it into the dip and pulling the soft meat off the underside of the leaf with the front upper teeth. Discard the leaves and do NOT throw them down the garbage disposal unless you want to spend hours trying to pull strings of artichoke back out of a jammed disposal. When the choke appears, remove it carefully with a spoon and discard. It is called a *choke* for a reason, and you don't want to get it caught in your throat. Enjoy the rich heart and stem.

HERB POPOVERS

Have all ingredients at room temperature.
Preheat oven to 450 degrees. Make sure the popover or muffin tin is well-oiled, and then place it in the oven to get it piping hot before adding the batter.
Blend together in a mxing bowl:

> 3 eggs, slightly beaten
> 1 t. safflower oil
> 1-1/4 cups raw milk (or reconstituted powdered)
> 1 cup wholewheat flour, sifted
> 3/4 t. sea sat
> 1/4 t. marjoram
> 1/4 t. thyme
> 1/4 t. mace
> 1 t. fennel seeds
> 1 t. instant granulated onion

Pour batter into the HOT muffin cups, filling them nearly full. Return tins to oven at once and bake at 450 degrees for 30 minutes; then at 350 degrees for 15 minutes longer. DO NOT OPEN the oven until you are ready to remove the popovers. No peeking!

HINTS: Popovers are lighter than muffins, because of the high oven heat, the liberal use of eggs, and the beating of air into the mixture. The batter is thin.

Popovers should be baked in hissing-hot, very well oiled tins. Overbeating will reduce the volume

The oven must be up to 450 degrees when the popovers first go in or they will not rise.

If the children object to too strong a flavor, it is probably the fennel seeds they don't like. Just eliminate them.

APPLE BETTY

Mix thoroughly with fingers:

> 1 cup wheat germ
> 1/3 cup raw honey
> 2 t. apple pie spice
> 1/4 cup powdered milk
> 2 t. cinnamon
> 2 T. butter

Sprinkle half this mixture onto bottom of oiled 8 inch by 8 inch pan. Wash and slice 5 apples. Dribble and dab over the apples:

1/2 cup soy flour
1 T. butter
1/3 cup raw honey
1 t. blackstrap molasses
1/4 lemon, juice of
pinch sea salt

Stir. Place in casserole and cover with remaining crumb mixture. Bake at 375 degrees for 30 minutes, or steam over simmering water, covered, for same length of time. When apples are tender the dessert is done. Serves four generously.

DAY FOURTEEN

MENU: *Delicious Pork Chops*

Lemon Parsley Potatoes

Spinach

Raw Applesauce

Apple Cottage Pudding

DELICIOUS PORK CHOPS

Season 6 pork chops with: paprika, seasoned salt (or Spike) and salt and pepper.

Brown in oil. Then bake in glass or stainless pan at 200 degrees until done. Meanwhile, sautee in 1/4 cup butter or olive oil:

1/4 pound fresh mushrooms
1/4 onion, thinly sliced

Sprinkle with garlic powder. Add diced, fresh parsley or parsley flakes, and paprika and set aside.

About five minutes before you're ready to serve, place this mixture over the top of the chops.

OPTIONAL: a miniature of dry vermouth or red wine poured over the mushroom mixture while it is warming will cut the oil and enhance the flavor.

WE ARE NOT RECOMMENDING pork, since there is a great deal of controversy regarding its health value. While it has the highest usable protein value of any meat and is high in thiamine, it is claimed by some to be hard on the liver because of the toxins carried in the fat which liver must detoxify. Others claim that no matter how well pork is cooked it still can retain live worms which then infest the body of the consumer. The choice is up to you. We definitely DO NOT recommend ham or bacon unless it is home-cured, since sugar and nitrates are used in most commercial curing processes.

LEMON-PARSLEY POTATOES

Cut up into quarters fresh potatoes, and steam them, unpeeled, until cooked through. Place in serving dish and top with generous amounts of butter, sea salt, the juice of a fresh lemon, and diced, fresh parsley or parsley flakes.

SPINACH

Wash leaves and steam over simmering water until limp but still bright green. Put into serving bowl and add lemon, sea salt and butter to taste.

RAW APPLESAUCE

Wash, core but do not peel 4 medium apples. Place in blender with:

    1/8 cup lemon juice
    1/2 cup raw honey

Blend. Serve.

APPLE COTTAGE PUDDING

This is a rich and sweet pudding made without sugar. It has the texture of plum pudding—almost cake-like. Mix:

    2 T. butter
    6 T. sorghum
    2/3 cup raw honey
    1 cup wheat flour
    1/4 t. sea salt
    1/2 t. vanilla
    2 tart apples, chopped or grated
    1/3 cup oil
    1 fertile egg
    1-1/2 t. baking powder

1/2 cup raw milk
dash cinnamon

Melt the 2 T. butter and pour into greased 1½ quart casserole, or put butter into dish and melt in preheating oven or over steaming water.

Mix apples with sorghum and spread into bottom of pan. Mix and cream the oil and honey, add the egg and beat well. Sift together flour, baking powder and salt, and add alternately with the milk. Add vanilla and cinnamon last and pour over the apple mixture in the casserole. Bake at 350 degrees for 40 to 45 minutes, or steam the same length of time over simmering water.

TOPPING

Whip 1 cup plain yogurt mixed with 2 T. sorghum and ¼ t. ginger. Pour over top of each serving and sprinkle with allspice.

DAY FIFTEEN

MENU: *Chicken with Artichoke Heart*

Basque Tomatoes

Sliced Cumcumber Salad

Banana Nut bread

If cucumbers are not in season, substitute with Sunshine Salad.

CHICKEN WITH ARTICHOKES

1/2 lb. mushrooms, sliced
2 packages (9 oz. size)
artichokes hearts OR 1 jar marinated artichoke hearts, drained[13]
1 cup vegetable or chicken stock
2 T. arrowroot
1/4 cup alfalfa sprouts
4 lbs. chicken pieces
1-1/2 cups sherry[14]

---

13. Save marinade from artichokes and use in salad dressings.

14. Sherry is optional. It makes the dish richer and more gourmet, but does add some sugar.

3 T. stock
1/2 t. vegesal

Saute the mushrooms until tender. Remove from pan. Brown chicken, add sea salt, pepper, vegesal and dash of paprika. Next add artichoke hearts, sherry, 1/2 cup stock, and mushrooms. Cover and simmer 30 minutes or until meat is tender.

Remove chicken, artichokes and mushrooms from the pan, and in the liquid remaining in the pan add arrowroot that has been mixed with the 2 T. stock. Cook until gravy is thickened, and pour over meat and artichokes. Add sprouts very last so they do not cook.

This is also good served with whole wheat, barley, vegetable noodles or brown rice.

SLICED CUCUMBER SALAD

Blend together:

3/4 cup cider vinegar
1/2 cup water
2 T. honey
1 onion, sliced
2 cucumbers, sliced
1/4 lb. fresh mushrooms, sliced
4 peppercorns

Marinate 3 to 4 hours. Add salt after salad is served. Save and refrigerate marinade for future use, or add to your next salad dressing.

DAY SIXTEEN

MENU: *Halibut Oven-bake*

Salad

Whole Wheat Rolls or Spoon Bread

HALIBUT OVEN-BAKE

In glass pan place one halibut steak. Dribble juice of 1/2 lemon over it and dribble 1 t. olive oil over top. Season with sea salt, kelp and garlic powder.
Surround fish with:

grated carrots, sprinkled with cinnamon
grated or diced celery, sprinkled with vegesal
potatoes, cooked and sliced, seasoned with onion
salt and Spike
onion slices, salted

Salt all ingredients. Drip more olive oil over the potatoes
and vegetables (or use butter), cover, and bake at 200 degrees
until fish is flaky and carrots are cooked (about 30 minutes).
Before serving, cover fish with chopped, fresh parsley or
parsley flakes.
Serves 2.

DAY SEVENTEEN

MENU: *Bar-B-Que Beef Shortribs*

Waldorf Cabbage Salad

Cheese Muffins

Corn on the Cob

BAR-B-QUE SHORT RIBS

Use 2 ribs per person for this dish. Place meat in a stainless
baking or glass baking dish and bake in very slow oven (150
degrees) for 6 hours, or steam over simmering water. When
cooked through and tender, remove ribs from drippings and
reserve drippings for stock. Brush ribs with barbeque sauce
and sea salt and grill over charcoal.

BAR-B-QUE SAUCE

To 1/2 cup tomato sauce add:

juice of one lemon wedge
1 clove garlic, crushed
1/4 t. rosemary
1/4 t. sweet basil
dash honegar

Mix well and brush onto meat. Grill.

CORN ON THE COB

Steam corn over simmering water until water droplets form
on kernels. Serve immediately with butter, sea salt and Spike.

DAY EIGHTEEN

MENU: *Escabeche*

Fresh Vegetable Plate

Oven Fresh Whole Wheat Bread or Rolls

Carob Fudge Pie

ESCABECHE

Escabeche is a cold, marinated cooked fish that is common in Peru and Panama, and we suspect in neighboring countries. This meal can be fixed ahead of time.

> 2 pounds fillet of flounder, or turbot or other white fish
> cider vinegar to cover
> 3 T. whole wheat flour
> 3 T. oil
> 3 cloves garlic, minced
> 3 T. lemon juice
> 1/3 cup fresh orange juice
> 3 T. chives, minced, or 1/2 onion, chopped
> 1/4 t. coriander seeds, ground
> 1/4 t. sea salt
> 1 t. dulse, minced or kelp (both at health food stores)
> 1 T. food yeast or fragilis

Arrange fillets in shallow dish. Cover with vinegar. Marinate for 10 minutes. Drain fish and dredge in flour. Heat oil and saute fish briefly. Put back into shallow dish. Mix remaining ingredients in a bowl and pour over fish. Marinate in refrigerator for 24 hours. Serves 6.

VEGETABLE PLATE

Cover a large platter with Romaine or butter lettuce and drop a large mound of potato salad in the center. Surround with:

> cucumbers, sliced
> green onions
> zucchini, sliced
> carrot sticks

radishes
fresh mushrooms
celery sticks
tomato wedges

Season with salt, pepper and vegesal. Provide a dip for them:

BLEU CHEESE DRESSING DIP

Blend together with fork:
3/4 cup mayonnaise
1/4 cup plain yogurt
1/8 t. sea salt
1/8 t. white pepper
1/4 cup crumbled bleu cheese
1 t. Worchestershire Sauce (optional)
1/8 t. garlic powder
1T. lemon juice

Makes one cup.

CAROB FUDGE PIE

Make pie crust as described on page 144. Prebake.
Double the carob pudding recipe and pour into prebaked crust. Top with chopped nuts and unsweetened coconut.

DAY NINETEEN

MENU: *Deviled Short-Ribs*

Carrots

New Potatoes

Salad

Apple Pie

DEVILED SHORT RIBS

5 to 6 pounds beef short ribs
1/4 cup oil
1 t. cayenne pepper
2 cups chopped onions
2 T. horseradish
1-1/2 T. dry mustard

1 T. sea salt
2 beef bouillon cubes[15]
2 T. Worchestershire Sauce
1 T. Tamari or Kikkoman Soy Sauce

In large Dutch oven over medium heat brown ribs in oil, OR steam on rack over simmering water, covered. Stir remaining ingredients and 1-1/2 cups stock in and around ribs. If you steam them, you already have good meat stock to use for the 1-1/2 cups liquid.

Cover pan and cook over low heat about 2-1/2 hours until ribs are fork-tender. Serve with liquid, or remove ribs, and serve gravy separate. The gravy is very thin, and if you prefer it thicker, add 1 T. arrowroot and follow usual procedure for making gravy.

CARROTS

Wash and scrub, slice or grate, and steam until tender. Serve with lots of butter, sea salt and pepper.

NEW POTATOES

Scrub, and steam unpeeled. Serve with butter, sea salt and pepper.

DAY TWENTY

MENU: *Chicken Teriyaki*

          Brown Rice or Potato Salad

          Asparagus, Broccoli, or Artichoke

          Sunshine Salad

CHICKEN TERIYAKI

Marinate cut-up pieces of chicken:

    2/3 cup tamari or Kikkoman soysauce

---

15. Bouillon cubes and Worchestershire both have some undesirable ingredients. But we feel that used sparingly and only occasionally in a good diet that they are acceptable. Serves 6.

1/4 cup white wine or sake[16]
2 T. honey
1/2 t. ginger
1 clove chopped garlic

Marinate at least one hour. Six to eight hours is better. The longer you leave it, the stronger the flavor will be. It can even be left overnight.

Bake in marinade, uncovered, at 200 degrees until tender—about one hour. Baste from time to time. When done, remove chicken to platter and put marinade in pitcher to be dribbled over the rice, OR char-grill the meat. Heat the sauce and serve with the rice.

Chicken teriyaki makes a very good cold picnic meat.

ASPARAGUS

Wash. Break off the tough bottoms of the stalks. They will *give* under your pressure at just about the right place. Save these bottoms for stock. Asparagas stock is one of the tastiest. Steam the asparagas over simmering water until tender. Serve with plenty of butter, sea salt and pepper.

DAY TWENTY-ONE

MENU: *Portuguese Fish*

Fried Rice

Green Salad

Apple Sundae

PORTUGUESE FISH

Saute in olive oil: (Use amounts according to your taste)

---

16. Sake will give the authentic teriyaki flavor of the Hawaiian and Japanese foods. We used white wine many years for this recipe, and found when we visited Japan that the flavor wasn't quite right. The difference was the sake. Apparently the white wine was an American adaptation.

diced onion
diced garlic
diced celery
sliced raw mushrooms

Place in bowl, along with:

2 cut-up green peppers
4 cup-up fresh tomatoes OR
1 large can stewed tomatoes

Season to taste with:

cayenne
paprika
Italian Seasoning OR
rosemary, oregano, sage, thyme
sea salt

Pour tomato juice to cover over these ingredients, cover and set aside.

Place cut up fish (use amount needed) or turbot, halibut or sole in baking dish with olive oil to cover the bottom. Sprinkle fish with lemon. Bake at 250 degrees for 30 minutes. Pour mixture of vegetables over top and continue baking, uncovered, until fish is done. Before serving, top with diced parsley and alfalfa sprouts.

This is a good company meal, and goes well with black beans and rice. It is inexpensive, very filling, and somewhat unusual.

FRIED RICE

In stainless skillet saute over low heat in good oil:

1 small onion, diced
1/2 cup water chestnuts (optional) or sliced Jerusalem artichokes
1/4 lb. fresh mushrooms, sliced
1/4 cup wheat sprouts
1/4 cup chopped nut meats

Add:

2 cups cooked brown rice
2 t. sea salt
1 t. soy sauce
dash Spike

Stir and warm through. Just before serving add two beaten eggs and stir through rice. When eggs are solidified, rice is ready to serve. Top with diced tops of green onions, or as an alternative when onions are not available, serve rice with fresh lemon wedges to be squeezed over top of rice.

APPLE SUNDAE

In individual dishes place spoonful of plain yogurt, top with homemade applesauce and wheat germ nuggets.

HOMEMADE APPLESAUCE

Use your favorite recipe, substituting honey for the sugar and leaving the apples unpeeled.

DAY TWENTY-TWO

MENU: *Stuffed Green Peppers*

Cheese Muffins

Mixed Melon Salad

Green Salad

STUFFED GREEN PEPPERS

Brown one pound ground meat (lamb, beef or turkey) in skillet. If you choose beef, try to mix with ground beef heart or kidney.
Add:

> 1 medium onion, chopped
> 1/4 cup cashews and 1/4 cup almonds, chopped
> OR
> 1/4 cup sunflower seeds and 2 T. sesame seeds
> 2 T. wheat germ
> 2 t. sea salt
> 1/4 t. kelp
> 1 T. parmesan cheese
> 1/4 t. cayenne
> 1 t. fragilis or food yeast
> pinch each of rosemary, basil, poultry seasoning and kelp

Steam peppers above water just until warm through. Stuff with meat mixture if it is hot. OR if the mixture is cold, stuff peppers before steaming. Top with paprika, black pepper and wheat germ nuggets before serving.

ALTERNATE STUFFING: Mix left-over brown rice with chopped onion, mushrooms, chopped celery and a small can of tomato sauce. Season with a pinch of sea salt, honegar, Italian Seasoning and cook as above.

DAY TWENTY-THREE

MENU: *Pot Roast and Steamed Wheat*

          Yorkshire Pudding

          Brussels Sprouts

          Green Salad

POT ROAST

In hot, oiled roasting pan brown meat. When brown on both sides, top with one grated onion and one large, grated carrot. Add two cups stock, cover and cook very slowly until done. Water or stock should simmer, not boil. If you bake it in the oven, adjust the heat to 165 degrees and cook for 20 hours.

When meat is tender, remove to platter and keep warm. Take drippings left in pan off the heat, add 1 T. arrowroot for each 2 cups stock drippings. Season with sea salt, and Spike to taste. Stir and put back over low heat, stirring occasionally until gravy is thickened. Add pepper and serve over Yorkshire pudding, steamed wheat or steamed triticali. (You may wish to strain out the carrots and onions used to season the cooking meat. We prefer to leave them in the gravy.) Optional: add fresh sliced mushrooms to the gravy.

YORKSHIRE PUDDING

Have all ingredients at room temperature.

          3 fertile eggs
          1-1/2 cups raw milk
          1 t. sea salt
          1-1/2 cups whole grain flour
          1/2 cup butter
          1/2 t. low sodium baking powder

Combine eggs, milk, salt and flour. Beat with beater until smooth and well-blended. Melt butter in 9x13x2 inch pan. Pour batter into hot buttered pan. Bake at 425 degrees for 20 minutes, then reduce heat to 350 degrees and bake for 20 to 25 minutes until brown and crusty. Don't open oven door until pudding is done.

You may use the meat juices from the roast in place of the butter, or along with the butter. Any extra juices can be spooned over the pudding. The pudding should be high, with a hole in the center.

BRUSSELS SPROUTS

Peel off any yellowing leaves, and wash thoroughly. Steam over simmering water until tender but still green. Serve with butter, sea salt and pepper.

Adele Davis says that:

In experiments where identical roasts were cooked at different oven temperatures to the same degree of doneness, roasts cooked for 20 to 24 hours were preferred in 100 per cent of the taste tests to roasts cooked in three hours or less. Although the cooking time seems startling at first, the meat is so amazingly delicious, juicy, tender, sliced so beautifully, and shrinks so little that meats cooked at higher temperatures no longer taste good to you...In slow roasting, the oven temperature is set approximately at the tamperature you want the meat when it is done....It cannot burn; it needs no watching; vitamins and proteins cannot be harmed at such low heat; almost no fuel is needed to cook it. One might say that it cooks itself.[17]

She does recommend searing it first before such slow cooking in order to kill surface bacteria.

DAY TWENTY-FOUR

MENU: *Spanish Veal*

             Basque Vegetables

             Basque Tomatoes

             Wheat Sesame Biscuits

---

17. Adele Davis, *Let's Cook It Right*, p. 56.

SPANISH VEAL[18]

This is one of the most common meat dishes of Spain. Marinate veal at least four hours or overnight in milk to cover the bottom of the marinade dish. Add 2 cloves crushed garlic. Turn meat occasionally. Drain at least one half hour before cooking. Brown veal in skillet with 2 T. olive oil. When it is tender and just slightly pink inside, it is done. Remove to platter, sprinkle with juice of lime or lemon, salt and pepper, and serve.

BASQUE VEGETABLES

Wash, but don't peel desired number of potatoes. Cut into quarters and steam over simmering water. Wash and cut off tips of green beans. When potatoes are almost cooked, add beans, and steam together until potatoes are tender and the beans are tender but still bright green. Remove to serving dish, sprinkle generously with fresh lime or lemon juice and then olive oil. Don't be afraid to use too much oil and lime. The juice that collects at the bottom of the dish will be dribbled over the potatoes when served.

WHEAT SESAME BISCUITS

> 1 cup wheat flour
> 2-1/2 t. low sodium baking powder
> 1-1/2 T. oil
> 1/3 to 1/2 cup water
> 1 T. raw honey
> sesame seeds and oil

Mix together all ingredients except seeds and sesame oil. Fill one small bowl with the seeds and another with the oil. Roll the biscuits into balls, then roll in the oil and the seeds. Bake on baking sheet at 400 degrees for 15 minutes. Serve with butter and honey.

Leftover oil and seeds, along with seeds that fall off onto the baking sheet during baking can be mixed together and added to tomorrow's breakfast eggs or dinner gravy.

---

18. Lamb may be substituted where veal is not available.

DAY TWENTY-FIVE

MENU: *Quick Chicken*

French Onion Triticali

Green Salad

Sliced, Honey Tomatoes or Buttered Carrots

Flan, or Custard

QUICK CHICKEN

Place cut-up chicken, as much as you need, into baking dish and bake at 250 degrees over for two hours.

One-half hour to one hour before serving, melt in saucepan 1/2 cup butter or olive oil, or a combination of both with generous amount of crushed garlic. Season meat with salt, pepper, vegesal, paprika, lemon juice, and poultry seasoning, and pour the melted butter over top. Dribble some of the chicken drippings over top. Continue baking until meat is tender, basting occasionally.

If you have some precooked potatoes or other vegetables, put them alongside the chicken the last 15 minutes and baste. Top with chopped parsley before serving.

FRENCH ONION TRITICALI

Steam triticali (or wheat) overnight. To 2 cups triticali add:

1/2 cup chopped onions
2 Cloves chopped garlic
1 cup beef bouillon or beef stock

Cover grain with the stock and steam until grains are warm, soft, but not popped open. About 8 hours. When grain is steamed properly, mix together:

1-1/2 cups meat drippings or meat stock
2 T. powdered arrowroot
2 cups stock
1 can French onion soup
1 medium onion, sliced

Cook over low heat like gravy. When thickened, add steamed triticali and warm through.

SLICED HONEY TOMATOES

Over fresh, sliced tomatoes sprinkle wheat germ and sesame seeds and dribble raw honey over top.

CUSTARD

3 eggs, beaten
1/3 cup raw honey
1-1/2 cups hot milk
1/2 t. sea salt
1 t. vanilla

Beat together. Pour into custard cups, pie shell, or pie tin. Bake at 425 degrees for ten minutes, then at 375 degrees for 15 to 20 minutes, or until a knife inserted into the middle comes out clean.

If you want plain custard, sprinkle nutmeg over the top before baking.

FLAN

This is an adaptation of Spanish flan, because we use honey rather than sugar, and it is sweeter than the plain custard.

In the bottom of the custard dish or custard cups put a tiny bit of honey with a drop of molasses. Mix together, and use enough to lightly cover bottom of pan. Pour custard into pan and bake. When done, turn custard upside down onto plate and you'll have Spanish flan, a national dessert of Spain and many Spanish American countries.

VARIATION: Before serving regular custard, spread the top with a honey base jam of plum or other tart jam. This is especially good as a topping for custard pie, makes it look colorful and festive, and the tartness of the jam contrasts perfectly with the rich sweetness of the custard, the one complementing the other.

DAY TWENTY-SIX

MENU: *Baked Halibut*

Squash

Egg Foo Yung

Green Salad

BAKED HALIBUT

This is a quick, very high-protein dinner.
Brush baking dish with butter.
Place halibut in dish and top with dab of butter. Bake at 200 degrees. When fish is almost done, season to taste with:

> more butter
> fresh chopped parsley
> lots of paprika
> lime or lemon juice
> vegesal
> minced onions
> sea salt
> kelp

Finish baking until fish can be flaked with a fork.

SQUASH

Cut up yellow squash like acorn squash into quarters and steam cook over simmering water until soft. Remove from heat and scrape squash from skins into bowl. Add generous amounts of:

> butter
> sea salt
> pepper
> cinnamon
> pumpkin pie spice
> dab of honey

Mix well and serve.
NOTE: Or steam bake in oven. Place water to cover bottom of baking dish or cookie sheet. Place cut squash halves upside down (skins on top) on sheet and bake until done.
For a crispy texture add chopped pumpkin seeds or some sunflower seeds, and/or chopped nuts.

EGG FOO YUNG

Sautee in soy oil over medium heat until warm but still crisp:

> mung bean sprouts
> onions

Season to taste with sea salt. Beat one egg per person and add to the above. Add dash of soy sauce and cook very slowly. Turn once with a spatula. Serve with soy sauce.

DAY TWENTY-SEVEN

MENU: *Saurbraten*

        Spaetzle

        Sweet-Sour Red Cabbage

        Buttered Green Beans or Peas

MILWAUKEE DUTCH SAURBRATEN

This saurbraten was served, with sugar instead of honey, in a restaurant owned by a German, Otto Schottz, at the turn of the century in the German settlement Watertown, near Milwaukee, Wisconsin.[19]

Marinate 4 lbs. of beef (roast, chuck, or rump) for 5 days to two weeks in:

> 1 cup cider vinegar
> 1/2 cup honey
> 3 cups water
> 1 sliced onion
> 3 T. mixed whole spices.
> 1 t. sea salt

Turn in marinade once a day. When ready to bake, pour off the marinade and save. Wipe the meat dry and roast at 300 degrees until nearly done. Sprinkle with 1/2 cup honey and continue roasting until browned. Watch closely, since honey will brown more quickly than sugar, and you may have to lower your oven temperature. Pour marinade over the roast, or strain it first and pour it over. Sprinkle over top:

---

19. Saurbraten means "sour meat," and if you want a really authentic German flavor, use only ¼ cup honey in the marinade. This is usually a little too sour for American tastes, and we prefer the old Wisconsin German version.

    The meat will "sour" faster if you use the good cider vinegar as recommended in this book, and if the meat is left at room temperature rather than refrigerated.

2 t. ginger, ground
1 t. molasses
1/2 cup unsulfured raisins
1/2 cup red wine

Bake until meat is tender. Thicken gravy slightly with arrowroot. Serves 6.

SWEET SOUR RED CABBAGE

Grate one small head red cabbage. Steam over simmering water, or cook at low heat with just a touch of water in bottom of heavy stainless pan. When tender but still crisp (10 to 15 minutes at the most), remove to serving dish, add salt, butter, pepper, and honegar to taste.

SPAETZLE, OR GERMAN EGG DUMPLINGS

Beat 2 eggs. Combine them with:

1-1/2 cups whole wheat flour
1/2 cup stock
1/2 t. sea salt
1/4 t. low sodium baking powder
small grating of nutmeg

Beat well. Drop small bits of batter from a spoon into simmering, salted stock. Spaetzen should be light and delicate. If it seems too heavy, add stock to the batter. Simmer until they rise to the surface of the liquid. Drain and place in dish for serving.

BUTTERED GREEN BEANS

Wash, and cut off tips of beans. Slice beans to your preference, or leave whole. Steam over simmering water. When tender but still green, remove to serving dish. Squeeze juice of half a lemon over top, butter generously, and salt and pepper to taste. Mix and serve. (Optional: add sliced raw almonds.)

DAY TWENTY-EIGHT

MENU: *Pizza*

          Fruit Delight

          Yogurt Sundae

PIZZA

CRUST: In 1 T. milk dissolve 2 oz. yeast, and add:

1/4 cup reconstituted powdered milk
1/4 cup olive oil
1 t. sea salt
3 cups whole wheat flour, finely ground.

Knead for 20 minutes. Let rise for 3 hours. Then roll dough onto pizza tin or baking sheet, pinching up a collar around the edges to hold the filling. This will make the crust crisp and crunchy. (Prebaking the crust at 350 degrees will make the crust crispier.)

TOPPING: Distribute evenly over the crust:

1 can pitted black olives, sliced[20]
1 large onion, diced
1/2 lb. mushrooms, sliced[21]
1-1/2 lbs. monterrey jack cheese
1 lb. ground turkey, browned and drained, and seasoned well with Italian seasoning.

Cover this with two 10 oz. cans of tomato sauce)or less, if you prefer a less tomato-y pizza), and sprinkle over top:

sea salt
paprika
rosemary
parmesan cheese
food yeast
wheat germ
pepper
Italian Seasoning
Bouquet Garni (at supermarkets

Bake at 350 degrees until cheese is melted and crust is done.

------

20. Make sure the olives have no preservatives or colorings added. The most likely place to buy them is in an Italian delicatessen specialty shop.

21. For a richer flavor, sautee the mushrooms first in olive oil.

Some prefer to make individual pizzas on fried corn tortillas.

FRUIT DELIGHT

Combine pineapple chunks (fresh or unsweetened canned), chopped nuts, raw, unsweetened coconut and sliced bananas.

YOGURT SUNDAE

Place unflavored yogurt in individual bowls. Top with homemade fruit sauce such as applesauce, made with honey, or with fruit in season, sliced and honeyed. Over top sprinkle chopped nuts, wheat germ nuggets, and/or unsweetened coconut.

DAY TWENTY-NINE

MENU: *Turkey*

Dressing

Pumpkin

Green Salad

Wheat Sesame Baking Powder Biscuits

TURKEY THAT'S DIFFERENT

Heat oven to 400 degrees. When hot, turn oven to 200 degrees and place in it a 15-pound turkey. I use a broiler pan instead of a roaster. Leave uncovered, and season with sea salt. Cook until done—up to ten hours.

Meanwhile, sautee in one-half cup each olive oil and butter:

> large raw mushrooms, sliced
> scallions or green onions
> 2 to 4 cloves garlic, crushed
> rosemary

Season with sea salt and poultry seasoning. Add some of the juices from the cooking turkey. When mushrooms are saturated, but not fully cooked, remove from heat, and add juice and rind of 1/2 lemon, generous amounts of fresh, chopped parsley, and let stand.

Half an hour before serving, sprinkle turkey with more salt and poultry seasoning, and baste with mixture, being sure to add juices from the turkey. Baste as often as you like. Let bake remaining 30 minutes, or until done. Sprinkle more parsley over top, and serve using all the oils and juices from the pan in place of gravy, to be poured over meat when serving. (Don't thicken the juices.) .

For a variation you might add dry vermouth to the oil mixture.·

This is a juicy turkey, easy to make and different in flavor. Left-overs are delicious in rice flavored with the juices.

You may cook a three pound whole chicken the same way. Place small cooked potatoes and raw onions quarters around it, season, and treat as you did the turkey.

DRESSING

This is a healthy, filling, low-carbohydrate dressing with a fruity flavor. Use all fresh ingredients if possible

Cook giblets slowly, below 180 degrees, along with:

> bay leaf
> 1/4 t. thyme
> 1/2 t. sage
> diced garlic clove

Meanwhile, saute in oil:

> 1/2 cup sesame seeds
> 1/2 cup sunflower seeds
> 1 cup wheat sprouts
> 1 cup cut-up mushrooms (use the stems and sides from the mushrooms sliced for the turkey)
> 1 medium onion (more if you like onion), diced
> 4 pieces bacon, cut up (optional
> 1 large stalk celery, including leaves, diced

Season with:

> salt
> pepper
> Vegesal
> poultry seasoning
> 1/4 cup wheat germ oil (optional)

Add:

> 1 cup chopped fresh parsley
> 1/2 cup wheat germ
> 1-1/2 cups chopped nuts (use a variety)
> 1 diced tart apple, unpeeled
> cooked giblets, diced
> juice from cooking giblets
> homemade wheat bread in quantity desired

Mix together. If more juice is needed, use stock. Season with:

> 1/4 t. cinnamon
> 1/4 t. nutmeg
> 1/4 t. allspice
> salt to taste
> 1/2 t. Spike
> 1/2 t. poultry seasoning
> 1/2 t. garlic powder
> 1 fresh lemon, juice only

Stir all together and refrigerate. Bake separately from turkey in slow oven—200 degrees.

ALTERNATE DRESSING:

Saute in butter and olive oil:

> giblets
> onion slices
> lots of fresh mushrooms

Add:

> diced shallots and garlic
> hot turkey or chicken stock
> Spike
> salt
> Crumbled Northridge wheat berry bread

Add ingredients until dressing is soggy. Taste and adjust seasoning.

PUMPKIN

as a vegetable

Mix together:

> 3 cups cooked pumpkin
> 3/4 cup cream
> 1/3 cup butter
> nutmeg
> allspice
> cinnamon
> Pumpkin pie spice

Place in covered casserole dish in 200-degree oven until warm, or steam warm, or warm in heavy stainless saucepan over low heat.

DAY THIRTY

MENU: *Tacos*

Guacamole

Refried Beans

Steamed Tortillas

TACOS

In skillet brown 1-1/2 pounds ground turkey, lamb or beef. Add 1 can tomato sauce, 1 T. chili powder, and 1 t. honegar, with sea salt to taste. Cook until flavor works through. (You may prefer more chili powder.) When you are just about ready to eat, cover skillet bottom with corn oil. Place a corn tortilla[22] in the oil, adding the meat filling to the center of the tortilla. Quickly fold the tortilla over in half to form a half moon. The oil will soften the tortilla so that you can fold it, but if you wait too long it will be fried crisp and will tear rather than fold.

When tortilla is crisp on one side, turn over carefully and fry until crisp on second side. Remove from pan and drain on layers of paper towels. Salt, and keep warm in oven.

Serve these condiments at the table for everyone to dress his own Mexican Hot Dog:

> grated cheddar cheese
> diced fresh tomatoes

------

22. Buy tortillas made only with corn and water.

diced onions
coleslaw[23]

COLE SLAW

Grate 1/2 head cabbage, and add:

1/2 cup honegar
1/2 cup cider vinegar
1/4 cup water
peppercorns
1 t. sea salt
1 small onion, diced

Marinate at least 8 hours.

GUACAMOLE

2 ripe avocados
1/4 cup onion, diced finely
1 T. lime juice (or lemon)
3 cloves garlic, crushed
1 small can chili pepper (optional)
plenty of salt to taste

Mash avocados with fork, add other ingredients. Taste, adding more of any one ingredient until you get the flavor you want. It should be very full of strong flavors, rather than bland and lardy like our American-style Mexican restaurant kind.

Serve over lettuce, or use as topping on tacos, or as topping on rolled, steamed tortillas filled with refried beans.

REFRIED BEANS

Again, most Mexican restaurants in this country serve beans that are not refried, and are bland and starchy. We think we have the real flavor in these beans—the kind we ate with our breakfasts in Mexico and San Salvador.

---

23. In Mexico the tacos are served with tomatoes, onion and lettuce and mayonnaise along the side of the taco. You can make the salad with lettuce and mayonnaise dressing to be more authentic, but we have found that this combination highlights each flavor and we prefer the German-style cole slaw.

Cover bottom of heavy skillet with corn oil. Add left-over chili beans. Heat over low heat, stirring often and adding oil when the beans begin to stick, until they are dark brown—about four hours. Season generously with garlic powder and onion powder while cooking. Serve over steamed tortillas or fried tortillas, topped with cheese and guacamole, or roll up in steamed torillas, topped with guacamole.

HYPOGLYCEMICS should not have to worry about eating these if they are sure to use plenty of cheese, and eat all the vegetables. Corn, beans, and cheese are complementary, constituting a well-balanced protein meal. Of course, the beans must have been cooked over low heat, and should have been sprouted first.

SOME EXTRA MAIN DISHES

RED SNAPPER

Cut fish into small pieces. Heat oil in deep pan while you prepare batter.
Batter:

> 1/4 cup wheat germ
> 1 T. ground sesame seeds (optional)
> 3/4 cup whole wheat flour
> 1/4 cup soy flour
> 2 t. food yeast
> dash kelp
> 1/4 t. cayenne
> 1/2 t. paprika

Add beer or soda water to consistency desired. Deep fat fry. If you can get your family used to the taste, fry in olive oil. It is the only oil that doesn't become polysaturated when heated.

This batter can be used for other fish and for shrimp, as well as Japanese tempura. (For tempura, you might use 1/2 wheat and 1/2 rice flour rather than the wheat-soy combination above.)

FINNAN HADDY

Place cut-up pieces of finnan haddy in a stainless or a ceramic baking dish. Brush with butter. Squeeze half a lemon over the fish, dot with 1/4 cup butter and bake, uncovered, at 180 degrees until done, about one-half hour. Serve with beet greens, steamed and sprinkled with wine vinegar. Serve mashed potatoes with lots of melted butter to pour over top of potatoes and fish.

FANTASTIC SALMON STEAK

One of the problems with salmon steak is that it tends to be dry. We thought we were very clever to apply a Spanish tenderizing technique to the salmon which resulted in moist salmon. Pleased with ourselves, we told a retired commercial fisherman in San Francisco that we had discovered a way of cooking salmon that made it more moist than it was before cooking. He replied, "I know. Marinate it in milk first."

Marinate the salmon steak in milk, and 2 or 3 cloves of crushed garlic. Drain. Brush with olive oil, and grill or broil slowly. Before serving, sprinkle with lemon and sea salt and pepper, and top with chopped parsley.

Or top with MUSTARD BUTTER: Whip 1/4 cup butter, add diced parsley, 1/4 t. dry mustard, and whip again. Place dollop of mustard butter atop each steak.

PORCUPINE MEAT BALLS

1-1/2 lbs. ground beef, turkey, or lamb
1/2 cup raw brown rice
1 t. sea salt
1 medium onion, chopped
3 to 4 cloves garlic, diced
1 15 oz. can tomato sauce and 1-1/2 cups stock
OR: 1 cup stock and 1-1/3 cups tomato soup (No. 1 can)

Mix the ground meat and the rice, and roll into balls. Mix soup and stock and drop meat balls into the simmering liquid. Simmer 45 to 60 minutes. Just before serving add 1 cup alfalfa sprouts and stir them into the sauce. Serve over mashed potatoes, with a green salad.

SOUR CREAM SWEDISH MEATBALLS

1-1/2 lbs. ground lamb, turkey or beef
1 cup cooked brown rice
OR: 1/2 cup cooked rice and 1/2 cup wheat sprouts or steamed wheat
1 t. paprika
3/4 t. sea salt

1/4 cup diced onion
2 T. oil
1/2 cup stock
1 beef boullion cube
1 t. Worchestershire sauce
1 can cream mushroom soup[24]
1/2 cup yogurt
OR: 1/4 cup yogurt, and 1/4 cup real sour cream,
or 1 cup yogurt-kefir cheese
1/4 cup chopped parsley
1 t. garlic powder

Combine beef, rice, paprika, salt and onions and shape into balls. Brown in the oil. Place meat balls into 1-1/2 quart casserole. Drain fat from skillet combine stock, boullion cube, Worchestershire and mushroom soup until smooth. Add yogurt and pour over balls. Cover and refrigerate it if you are not cooking it immediately. Bake UNCOVERED at medium heat 45 minutes. Serves 6.

For a richer meat flavor you may want to leave the fat in the skillet when combining other ingredients.

This is an especially good hot dish for group get-togethers.

KIDNEY

1 beef kidney
2 onions, sliced
honegar
oil
1 can whole tomatoes (large size)
diced green pepper
2 cloves garlic, crushed

A pinch each of:

rosemary
thyme

---

24. Mushroom soup contains some undesirables, and hypoglycemics may not be able to tolerate it. It contains starch, sugar and undegerminated flour. A possible substitution is ½ c diced raw mushrooms, sauteed in butter, 1 c raw milk mixed with 1 T. arrowroot.

sweet basil
Italian Seasoning
sea salt to taste

Slice kidneys, removing the hard cartilage. Marinate with one onion in honegar for 24 hours, or overnight. Turn occasionally. Drain well. In oiled skillet brown kidney and the remaining onion. When meat is brown and onions are tender, add garlic, tomatoes, and spices. Cover and simmer until kidney is tender. Add the green pepper and cook until pepper is warm and tender but still somewhat crisp and green. Add black pepper and serve.

ALTERNATE KIDNEY

1 beef kidney
2 cans whole tomatoes
1 onion, diced
5 cloves garlic, sliced
1 t. rosemary
1 t. sweet basil
1 t. thyme
salt to taste

Cut 1 beef kidney into cubes, removing cartilage. Sautee in olive oil with onion. Add garlic, tomatoes, seasonings and cover. Simmer at least 4 hours.

Remember that flavor of organ meats can vary greatly. One time the kidney you buy may be mild—the next time it is strong. Try to use it when it is fresh, for a milder taste.

YOGURT CHICKEN

1 large chicken, cut-up
3 T. oil
2 onions, sliced
2 cups stock
juice of 1/4 lemon
3 T. arrowroot
1/4 t. sea salt
1 T. food yeast
2 t. tarragon
1 T. parsley, minced
1 pint plain yogurt

Brown chicken in oil, or brush with oil and broil lightly on each side. Sprinkle with:

> onion powder
> garlic powder
> poultry seasoning
> thyme
> sea salt

Arrange chicken in casserole, and surround it with the onions. Blend together stock arrowroot, salt, yeast, tarragon and parsley. Pour mixture over chicken and onions. Cover and bake at 200 degrees until tender, about two hours. Remove casserole from oven and pour out liquid, or remove chicken from liquid. Blend yogurt into liquid, and return chicken and liquid to casserole. Reheat if necessary. Serves 6.

SPECIAL MEATLOAF

Mix together:

> 2 lbs. ground turkey or lamb,
> OR: 2 lbs. combined heart, kidney and ground beef
> 1 onion, diced
> 1/2 cup tomato sauce
> 1/3 cup prepared mustard, or 1 T. dry mustard
> dash Worchestershire sauce
> 1 t. soy sauce
> 1-1/2 to 2 t. dry horseradish
> 2 t. sea salt
> 2 t. garlic powder
> 1/4 t. cayenne pepper
> 2 t. paprika
> 1/4 t. vegesal
> 1/2 t. kelp
> 1 cup parsley, diced
> 1/2 cup wheat germ
> 1 egg
> 1/4 cup recon powdered milk, not reconstituted
> 1 t. Bouquet Garni

Place in loaf pan and shape. Pour tomato sauce or A-1

Sauce[25] over top, lay on strips of green pepper, and squeeze juice of half a lemon over it all. Next put paper-thin slices of lemon on top and finally sprinkle with rosemary and Bouquet Garni or oregano. Bake at 350 degrees for 1-1/2 hours, or steam in pan over simmering water for same length of time.

MEATLOAF CASSEROLE

Use up the left-over meatloaf.

Place the saved liquid from cooking the meat loaf in an electric fry pan.

Cut up cooked potatoes and meat loaf into about one-inch chunks. Place in pan and start to brown.

Meanwhile, slice very thinly:

> 1 onion
> 1 turnip
> 2 stalks celery

Add to pan. Sprinkle with garlic powder:

> pepper
> Spike
> cayenne
> 2 t. vegesal
> salt to taste.

Pour over mixture 1 to 2 cups tomato juice. Cover, simmer until vegetables are done the way you like them.

STROGANOFF

Most of your meat recipes are easily converted to the "new way." Here we use yogurt, preferably homemade, with some cream that soured because it was not used quick enough. And we sneak some health-food fillers.

> 1-1/2 lbs. ground beef, lamb or turkey, or beef cut into thin strips
> 1 large onion, diced
> 1/4 lb. fresh mushrooms,
> OR: 1 can mushrooms, drained

---

25. Check the label on A-1 Sauce. You may not want to use it.

2 cloves garic, chopped
1 cup red wine
2 cups whole wheat or vegetable noodles
2 cups stock, mild flavored, or meat stock
2 beef boullion cubes
1 t. rosemary
1/4 cup alfalfa sprouts
1/2 cup diced fresh parsley
1 cup fresh yogurt or sour cream

In skillet brown meat, add onions, mushrooms and garlic. Sautee, adding more olive oil if needed. Add noodles, wine, stock, and beef boullion and spices. Stir, then cover. Cook one hour or until noodles and meat are cooked through. Add pepper, yogurt, parsley and sprouts just before serving.

Some people prefer draining the meat before adding the vegetables.

SWEET POTATO CHIPS

Peel the potatoes. It is okay to do with sweet potatoes because they don't have a mineral belt around the outside like regular potatoes. Slice very thin. Brown in hot olive oil until crisp on the edges. Drain on absorbent paper. Sprinkle with vegesal, and sea salt or onion salt, and Spike.

INDEX

A

Allburgers, 115
Apple Betty, 152
Apple Crisp, 145
Apple Sundae, 163
Applesauce,
  Homemade, 163
  Raw, 154
Artichoke, 151
Asparagus, 161

B

Beans,
  Refried, 108, 177
Beets and Greens, 143
Bread,
  Banana Nut, 124
  Corn, 128
  Garlic, 117
  Ginger, 127
  Graham Cracker Nut, 125
  Grapenut, 124
  Health, 141
  Jean's Whole Wheat, 129
  Peanut, 126
  Spoon, 128
  Whole Wheat Danish, 130
Broccoli, 147
Brussels Sprouts, 165
Butter,
  Basic, 119
  Cinnamon-Honey, 103
  Garlic, 140

C

Carrots and Parsnips, 132
Cereal, hot corn, 105
Chicken,
  with Artichokes, 155
  B-B-Q, 136
  Quick, 167
  and Rice, 148
  Teriyaki, 160
  Yogurt, 181
Chili Beans, 120
Chili Relish, 94
Cinnamon Carrots, 134
Cole Slaw, 177
Corn Cakes, 100
Corn on the Cob, 157
Custard, 168

D

Dressings, 174
  Alternate, 175
  Bleu Cheese, 159
  Catalina, 133
  Green Goddess, 151

E

Egg Foo Yung, 169
Eggs,
  Alfalfa Outter, 104
  Baked, 100
  German Dumplings, 171
  Huevos Rancheros, 109
  Sprouted Wheat, 108
Escabeche, 158

F

Farafa, 118
Finnan Haddy, 178
Fish,
  Grilled, 147
  Portuguese, 161
  Teriyaki, 133
Flan, 168
Fresh Fruit Dessert, 139
Frijoles Negros Con Arroz, 117
Fruit Delight, 173

G

Garlic Butter Toast, 119
Grains, steamed, 102

Green Beans, 171
Green Peppers, stuffed, 163
Guacamole, 177

H

Halibut,
   Baked, 169
   Oven-baked, 156
Hash Browns, 147
Herb Popovers, 152

K

Kidney, 180
   Alternate, 181

L

Lebanese Lamb Chops, 143
Liver for Liver-haters, 146

M

Mayonnaise, green, 134
Meat Balls,
   Porcupine, 179
   Sour Cream Swedish, 179
Meat Loaf,
   Casserole, 183
   Special, 182
Millet, 101
Milwaukee Dutch Saurbraten, 170
Mincemeat, raw, 94
Muffins,
   Cheese, 126
   Roman Meal, 125

O

Omelet
   American, 106
   French, 119
Onions, marinated, 118
Orange Spa, 90

P

Pancakes,
   Roman Meal, 105
   Sam's, 103
Panamanian French Toast, 101
Peach Melba, 149
Peas, buttered mint, 136

Pie,
   Carob Fudge, 159
   Crust, 144
   Graham Cracker, 137
   Mary's Pecan, 143
Pizza, 172
Pork Chops, 153
Pot Roast, 164
Potatoes,
   Lemon-parsley, 154
   Mashed, 132
Protein Shake, 91
Pudding,
   Apple Cottage, 154
   Carob, 116
   Pumpkin, 142
   Yorkshire, 164
Pumpkin, 175

R

Red Snapper, 178
Rice,
   Brown, 135
   Brown with Curry, 143
   Carrot Patties, 138
   Fried, 162
   Spanish, 139
Rolled Oats, 107
Rootbeer, 91
Rouladen, 131

S

Salad,
   Apricot-Nut, 114
   Banana Orange, 114
   Fresh Fruit, 113
   Green and Red, 148
   Lemon Green, 114
   Potato, 149
   Sliced Cucumber, 156
   Sliced Tomatoes and Onion, 114
   Spinach, 145
   Sunshine, 133
   Tuna-Avacado, 150
   Tuna, 115
   Waldorf Cabbage, 113
Salmon,
   Patties, 138
   Steak, 179

Sandwiches,
    Banana Peanut Butter, 111
    Egg, 111
    Grilled Sprout Cheese, 112
    Open-faced Egg Salad, 112
    Pumpkin Peanut Butter, 111
    Tomato-Avacado-Sprout, 112
    Tuna Sprout, 111
    Sardine, 111
Sauces,
    Bar-B-Que, 141, 157
    Curry, 141
    Honey-Butter, 127
    Steak, 141
    Sesame Salt, 135
Short Ribs,
    Bar-B-Que, 157
    Deviled, 159
Soup,
    Hunza Style Potato, 119
    Leek, 121
    Lentil, 122
    Pumpkin, 121
    Quick Vegetable, 124
    Split pea, 122
    Summer, 123
Sour Cream Horseradish, 141
Spaghetti, 144
Spanish Tortilla, 116
Spanish Veal, 160
Spinach, 154
Squash, 169

St. John's Brownies, 123
Strawberry Shortcake, 132
Stroganoff, 183
Sweet Potato Chips, 184
Sweet Sour Red Cabbage, 171
Swiss Fondue, 140

T

Tacos, 176
Tamales, 113
Teriyaki Shish-Kabob, 149
Tomatoes,
    Basque, 148
    Sliced Honey, 168
Triticali, French Onion, 167
Turkey that's Different, 173

V

Vanilla Chiffon Cream, 148
Vegetables,
    Basque, 166
    Mediterranean, 138
    Plate, 158
    Raw Plate, 115

W

Waffles,
    Berry, 120

Y

Yogurt Sundae, 173

Z

Zucchini, 147

—NOTES—

—NOTES—

—NOTES—

—NOTES—

—NOTES—